ISBN: 978-1-905540-57-0

Authors
Andrew Frapwell and Steven Caldecott

Project Lead Officer
Sue Wilkinson

Editor
Joanne Chapman

Designer
Ian Bolton

Front cover photograph © Alan Edwards
Back cover photograph © Mark Bullimore

The authors would like to thank the following for their contributions to this resource: Andrew Green (Outwood Grange Academy); Bryan Jones (University of Central Lancashire); Lawrence Dorman (Downend School); and Julia Harle and Lynn Hinder (Christian Malford School).

Published on behalf of afPE by

Association for Physical Education
Room 117
Bredon
University of Worcester
Henwick Grove
Worcester WR2 6AJ

Coachwise Ltd
Chelsea Close
Off Amberley Road
Armley
Leeds LS12 4HP

Tel: 0113-231 1310 Fax: 0113-231 9606
Email: enquiries@coachwise.ltd.uk
Website: www.coachwise.ltd.uk

90640:2

Foreword

Sometimes an educational book manages the leap between theory and practice. This one achieves something special; it links the theory, with the current and emerging policy context, with real practical examples from schools and classrooms. The style is engaging and the authors have used narrative and story carefully to exemplify some significant points.

It is a book that explores physical education examples and contexts, while, at the same time, delving into aspects of questioning or assessment. It sees teaching and learning as the multi-faceted exploration most people know it to be.

It is a book of numbers. It explains the nine gateways, the seven dimensions, the five components of personalised learning, the four 'Rs…along with QCDA's seven step development process to make it all happen.

More than anything, it is an absorbing read. It sheds light on the why and how of learning. Enjoy the book…and learn from it.

Mick Waters

Mick Waters
President of the Curriculum Foundation

Contents

Chapter 5: Learning to Learn Narratives

Chapter 6: Learning to Learn Practical Examples

List of Figures and Tables

Chapter 1: The Learning Milieu

Purpose

This chapter explores the rationale behind the writing of this book and its intended purpose. The concept of 'Learning to Learn' is outlined and a workable definition of the concept is provided. Aligned to this, the principles of Learning to Learn are explained and the importance of the area is highlighted in relation to curriculum developments in the UK.

Key Messages

- Learning can take place anywhere and in many different ways.
- Learning isn't always directly associated with, or driven by, good teaching.
- Learning is a process as well as a product.
- Learning can take place without memory.
- Learning is learnable.

The Learning Milieu

What is learning?

Read the author's example below.

'In the half-term holidays I purchased a cricket set for my children to play with. My eldest boy (six at the time) took control of the equipment and placed three stumps at the bottom of the garden and one stump at the top. He was batting of course; after all he was "in charge". My little girl, aged three, was given the role of bowler and my youngest boy, aged two, was told where to stand. My eldest was holding the bat as a left-hander (albeit with a right-handed grip), which meant my youngest boy was on the "off" side.

My daughter's initial attempts at bowling weren't that accurate and weren't reaching the vicinity of the target stumps, so her older brother instructed her to move the single stump closer. The next underarm effort made the distance, and the batter's left-handed, golf-like swing took the ball to his leg side, the opposite side of the wicket to which my youngest was standing. My little girl enthusiastically went to retrieve the ball, but my eldest, who had formed some idea of what cricket looked like from televised matches,

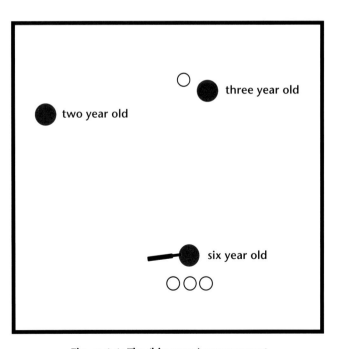

Figure 1.1: The 'big game' arrangement

informed my two year old that it was his job to collect the ball. "Why?" enquired my little girl, "I'm closest." The youngest, however, was already scooping up the ball and handing it back to the bowler before she could reason further. "Back over there in your position" the youngest was informed as my eldest banged the toe of the bat into the grass then changed his grip to the correct one with his left hand lower down the handle than his right. The youngest duly adopted his original position and my daughter bowled.

In the next few minutes a number of things happened. After a couple more deliveries my little girl informed my eldest boy that "I can do it now, so I'll put the stump back", and returned the stump to its original position further away from the wicket. My youngest, who by now had crossed to the opposite side of the wicket three times to collect the ball, made a decision to remain on that side.

For me, it was a eureka moment.

During my time at teacher training college in the 1980s we had been shown pairs cricket for use in lessons. Batters took turns in pairs to bat, another pair bowled, kept wicket and, usually, (depending on numbers) two more pairs fielded. After a designated amount of balls bowled everybody rotated positions and roles. To save time, the next pair in would fasten a cricket pad to their leading leg (a task made easier by the advent of Velcro instead of a leather buckle – which more often than not would have the pin missing). I used this arrangement on many occasions in my teaching career. Skills that I taught a group were practised in a pairs-game situation and everyone got a turn.

Yet, I had just witnessed learning without any teaching. Children as young as two and three were making decisions about the organisation of space that would challenge them (my three year old moving the single stump further away) and making decisions about the field placing according to the batter's strengths (my youngest changing sides). My eldest had changed his grip, which he informed me was "because it didn't feel right" and had led the organisation of the game as it was played. All the time I had been setting up pairs cricket for my pupils as shown in my teacher training, I had actually been minimising the opportunities for learning.'

This personal story serves to illustrate two key messages:

- Learning can take place anywhere and in many different ways
- Learning isn't always directly associated with, or driven by, good teaching.

Now, consider the following:

One of our colleagues is thinking of moving to Spain. She wanted to learn Spanish, so last year she bought a Spanish CD and began playing it in her car on long journeys. She practised saying words and phrases while imagining herself in Spain; on the beaches, ordering food and drink in the warm weather. She thought about what she would say in different situations, associated certain words with images to help her remember better and practised at times that helped her learn. (Unfortunately, the CD had a number of skips and today she can stutter in Spanish!)

As this example serves to illustrate, learning is not just about knowing things or knowing a lot, nor is it something that only happens in schools, colleges or universities. Learning is what the learner does to get better at something.

We have listed some statements on the next page to develop and maybe challenge your views of learning. Some of these are intentionally controversial. It might be worthwhile reading through and noting your individual reactions to these statements to ascertain where your current thinking about learning is. What do your colleagues think?

- Learning is the acquisition of knowledge through practice.
- Learning is a permanent change in behaviour.
- Developing physical skills is the most important aspect of our subject.
- Skills involving the use of muscular activity cannot be learnt without practice.
- Learning is knowledge of new facts and making sense of these from what is already known.
- Thinking about and discussing a particular decision in an activity slows down learning.
- The most important thing in learning physical education is remembering all of the teaching points about a skill.
- Some children will never learn in physical education and school sport – they are a lost cause.
- Playing or participating in any sport or activity uses a number of skills that have to be learnt by practising them in isolation.
- Successful practice is more effective than making mistakes.
- The amount of time spent engaging in a practice depends upon the complexity of the skills involved.
- Process skills (what we do to get better at something) are just as important as product skills.
- It is better to break down a complex skill, such as the lay-up shot in basketball, into separate components and practise them separately rather than practise the complex skill as a whole.
- The more difficult the skill appears to the learner, the more unlikely it is to be learnt.
- The more pointless a task or practice appears to the learner, the more unlikely it is to be learnt.
- If something cannot be learnt effectively enough to be done well, learners can still learn to enjoy doing it badly.
- The more mysterious something is; for example, problem-solving activities in outdoor and adventurous activities, the more unlikely it is to be learnt.

- Learners can only learn something new by relating it to things they already know.
- Learners need to perform a skill correctly to demonstrate learning has been achieved.
- A skill has only been learnt properly when it can be adapted successfully to unfamiliar situations.
- Learning should be more about making sense of something, such as analysing performance in a game, gymnastics or dance composition.
- Learning involves linking related parts of the subject matter; for example, the effects of exercise on fitness and health, to other subjects and the real world.
- Learning is about producing new knowledge by reflecting on experience.
- Physical education is really only about learning sports.
- Teachers need to tell learners everything they need to remember so they can perform tasks properly.
- We don't need to give teaching points about evaluating and improving performances, it is just a task that learners do.
- Skills can be learnt through games or game-like activity and we don't have to always practise them in drill-like situations.

These statements can be categorised into five broad paradigms of learning: Behaviourism; Cognitivism; Constructivism; Design-based; and Humanism[1]. Although psychologists and educationalists would exhaustively debate individual learning theories within these paradigms, it is generally considered that if learning has taken place, experience should have been used in some way. So, for example, conditioning a skill in a repetitive practice may result in a change in behaviour (sometimes referred to as **surface learning**), but the change may not have involved drawing upon experience (**cognitive processes**) to generate or construct new knowledge (sometimes called **deep learning**). This thinking, which underpins current educational reform and practice, is less concerned with overt behaviour than with changes in the

---

[1] Although this publication is not intended to provide an in-depth review of learning theories, it is worth describing an overview to promote thinking and awareness.

ways in which learners understand, experience, conceptualise and make sense of the world around them. Improving ways of remembering, practising, thinking, imagining, evaluating, deciding and so on, are all things we do to get better at something. These are often referred to as **process skills**.

Formal and informal learning

How do formal and informal learning promote deep or surface learning?

In the cricket story, it is unlikely the two year old was conscious that he was learning. This might be referred to as **informal** or **unplanned learning**. A simple question posed to him as to why he changed fielding position would potentially make him aware of his decision making. While he may have not been conscious of informal learning, he would have been conscious of the task he was engaging with, the same awareness as when he was acquiring the skill of walking. In the second example, the colleague is aware of the processes she can engage in to get better at learning Spanish. She is conscious of the learning going on – learning itself is the task. This situation is **formal learning**, although none of the more traditional teaching methods can be recognised. Formal learning in this context was not associated with traditional teacher-led methods, and this raises an anomaly. **It is in these teacher-driven, formal contexts, where content is viewed as something delivered to the learner and decisions are often controlled or heavily directed, that the greatest level of surface learning occurs.** We interfere with learner decisions, convinced we are helping them to something better – as in, perhaps, the pairs cricket example.

Learning and memory

To illustrate this point further, consider the following: how much do you remember of what you learnt in school? Could you remember how to replicate the energy cycle in science; the industry of the Massif Central between the Rhône-Saône valley and the basin of Aquitaine; how to order different foods in a foreign language; or what the acronym SOHCAHTOA stands for in mathematics? Unless you've used skills from school in your day-to-day life or profession, you may have trouble recalling the details. This is why, as educationalists, we draw on brain research and understand differences between learning and memory. Learning and memory are closely linked, but they are not the same thing as not all learning is transformed into lasting memories. Put very simply, learning is how you acquire new information about things and memory is how your brain stores that information over time. It is possible, therefore, to learn without memorising things, but it is impossible to memorise something without learning. For example, learners might be told to hold a badminton racket with a V-grip at the start of a lesson. Learners become good at retaining that information until the end of the session when the teacher asks 'how do you hold a badminton racket?' The following week the teacher asks the question again to recap and gets annoyed when learners do not remember. This is sometimes called **working memory**: it requires learning, but the methods used do not promote lasting memory. The methods used highlight information that is to be used for assessment; facts are associated without reflection as to why the racket is held that way, and the task is often perceived as an external imposition. These are characteristics of surface learning. The antithesis of this is when facts are related to everyday experience and other activities; for example, pincer grip, using our thumbs; frying pan grip; holding a glass tumbler or holding a hammer; links to golf, tennis and Wii sports are made and content is structured into a coherent whole. These are characteristics of deep learning and can impact on the extent to which you recall and remember things.

Okay, so if that broadly defines learning, what is Learning to Learn?

You could be forgiven for believing that every time phenomena in learning and teaching becomes 'completely' defined in educational literature, someone discovers or puts forward something which either does away with the previous concept or system, or expands it beyond recognition. So, at this early stage, be reassured that the area of Learning to Learn has been extensively researched and it is not just another programme innovation to be implemented by institutions. The former Department for Children Schools and Families (DCSF) made an undertaking to the profession that initiatives would not be introduced unless they had strong research backing[2]. In addition, the Learning to Learn concept should build on your existing knowledge and understanding of learning rather than replace it.

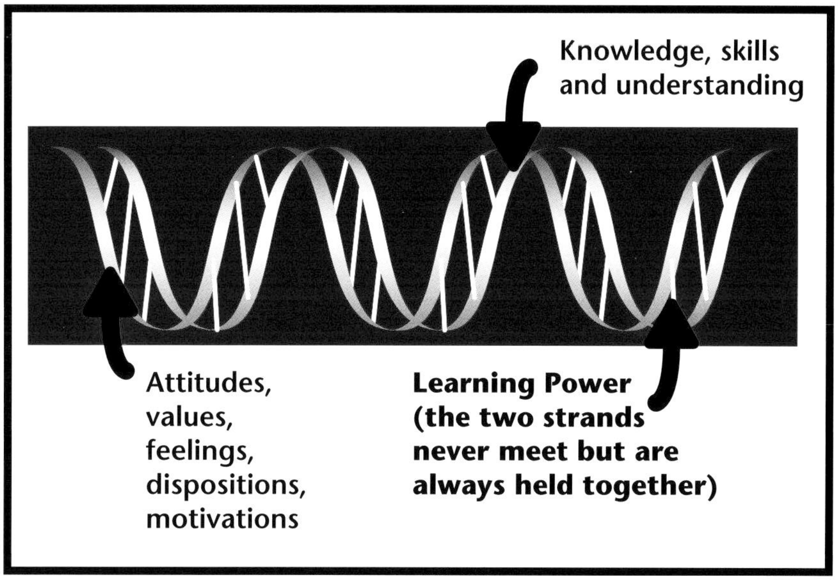

Figure 1.2: The double helix of learning

'Learning to Learn is the ability to pursue and persist in learning, to organise one's own learning, including through effective management of time and information, both individually and in groups. This competence includes awareness of one's learning process and needs, identifying available opportunities, and the ability to overcome obstacles in order to learn successfully. This competence means gaining, processing and assimilating new knowledge and skill as well as seeking and making use of guidance.

'Learning to Learn engages learners to build on prior learning and life experiences in order to use and apply knowledge and skills in a variety of contexts: at home, at work, in education and training. Motivation and confidence are crucial to an individual's competence.'

(Education Council, 2006)

Of particular note with regard to this definition of learning, is that it embraces learning theories from the five learning paradigms listed earlier (page 3). The acceptance,

rational adoption or rejection of this definition or elements of it will depend on your current values and understanding of learning. Suffice to say the changes to national curricula in England, Wales, Scotland and Northern Ireland (all implemented 2008) re-emphasised learning processes, contexts for learning, the importance of skills for life, skills of pursuance, persistence, independence and interdependence, and personal skills of organisation and motivation. In other words, government education departments embraced the Learning to Learn concept. Deakin Crick, Broadfoot and Claxton (2004, p. 250) promoted a process that helps young people become better learners and prepares them for a lifetime of learning. They use the term 'building learning power', which advocates 'a complex mix of dispositions, lived experiences, social relations, values, attitudes and beliefs that coalesce to shape the nature of an individual's engagement with any particular learning opportunity of individual students'.

This builds on the work of McGettrick (2002), who presents learning power as a double helical model (see Figure 1.2 above). Imagine the model to consist of a train

[2] Research into the Learning to Learn area is explored in more detail in Chapter 4.

> *"Ask your pupils how much sleep they are getting. Eight hours is still the figure we should aspire to."*

track with railway sleepers running perpendicular to the tracks and then twisted. One of the tracks represents knowledge, skills and understanding (the learning content that we engage learners with), and the other track represents learner attitudes, dispositions and motivations to the learning they are engaging with. These tracks run parallel, but without the sleepers they could begin to separate and become distant. The analogy here is that the learner becomes disaffected and disengaged with learning and progression, and achievement suffers. The railway sleepers or a learner's learning power can contribute to keeping these elements on track and powerfully linked. The term 'sleepers' is an appropriate one in this analogy, in that learning power often lies dormant and untapped in young people. We do our best for them, when in actual fact we could be getting learners to do a lot more for themselves.

The concept of Learning to Learn moves our thinking to a process of discovery about learning. If we understand learning and its various forms, then competencies and skills can be developed and used to help learners learn more effectively, and so become learners for life.

> *'At its heart is the belief that learning is learnable.'*

Raison d'être

Many schools have embraced the Learning to Learn concept but, all too often, physical education teachers have commented about the whole-school training they have received and how it has not always met their needs. When questioned, the event trainers have struggled to explain how Learning to Learn might be facilitated and how learner competencies might manifest in physical education lessons. There are plenty of classroom examples of Learning to Learn but few of what it might look like in physical education. The authors both share a deep-rooted

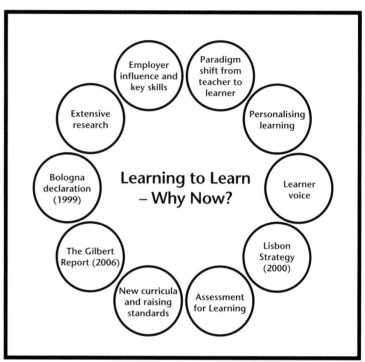

Figure 1.3: Key factors shaping and supporting the Learning to Learn approach in schools

interest and passion in terms of pedagogy, and have attended Early Lifelong Learning Inventory (ELLI) Learning to Learn consultant training at the University of Bristol. Their separate involvement with various Association for Physical Education (afPE) contracts and teacher needs led to afPE commissioning this Learning to Learn publication for physical education and school sport.

Figure 1.3 summarises the readiness factors that have formed the landscape for the advent of Learning to Learn. Personalising Learning, the Gilbert Report, Assessment for Learning (AfL) and Learner Voice are discussed in Chapter 2; extensive research and links to attainment (new curricula and raising standards) are introduced in Chapter 3 and engaged with further in Chapter 4; the remaining areas are introduced in Chapter 1, and all areas have further resources or reading referenced in the appropriate Further Reading sections. Chapter 5 presents four case studies (one primary, two secondary and one higher education institution). These are personal stories about Learning to Learn implementation and reflect a narrative about a process and moments in time. The final chapter highlights dozens of Learning to Learn ideas in practice, collated from physical education practitioners in England.

General Topography

To understand the current landscape it is necessary to follow the evolvement of the European Union (EU) and policy drivers in member state countries. There are two key summits that represent two sides of the same 'learning coin' and these are referenced to promote reader 'meaning making'. The two summits are:

- The Bologna Declaration 1999
- The Lisbon Strategy 2000.

The Bologna Declaration 1999

In 1999, education ministers from 29 different countries signed up to the Bologna agreement. This has recently risen to 46. The declaration aimed to establish a European Higher Education (HE) Area by 2010 and the objectives included the:

- adoption of a three-tier system of easily accessible and comparable degrees: Bachelors, Masters and PhDs
- establishment of a European credit transfer system
- promotion of mobility
- promotion of European cooperation in quality assurance
- promotion of the European dimension in HE
- lifelong learning
- involvement of students
- attractiveness and competitiveness of the European HE Area.

There have been further ministerial summits every two years, with work programmes and working parties established in the interim. These working parties have been linked to the eight Bologna objectives listed, and include groups on mobility, employability, qualification frameworks, lifelong learning, the social dimension, data collection and stocktaking, and the position of the European HE Area in the global context. Of particular interest to the professional sectors was the agreement that the 46 Bologna signatory countries had to develop national qualification frameworks, to be referenced against the Bologna three-tier structure. This convergence is already being noticed in the UK with, for example, the move towards the teaching profession becoming a Masters-level profession.

What the Bologna declaration has created is the infrastructure and opportunity for learner choice, clear learner pathways, mobility and accessibility to courses, learner involvement, employability and, perhaps most important of all, opportunity to engage in lifelong learning. This achievement, especially with reference to lifelong learning, takes on greater significance when viewed in conjunction with the Lisbon Strategy.

The Lisbon Strategy 2000

In Lisbon, the leaders of the EU member states decided the strategic goal for the next decade was for Europe to 'become the most competitive and dynamic knowledge-based economy in the world, capable of sustainable economic growth with more and better jobs and greater social cohesion' (European Council 2000, paragraph 5).

In addition to traditional economic measures, the need to invest in people was catered for, which included a series of measures related to Europe's education and training systems that paralleled with the Bologna declaration. This was the first time in the history of EU summits that education and training had been described as a major tool for implementing a strategic goal. Among the measures was the development of a European framework to define the new basic skills to be provided throughout lifelong learning (European Council, 2000, paragraph 26). By 2006 a set of eight competencies were developed that defined lifelong learning. These were:

- communication in the mother tongue
- communication in foreign languages
- mathematical competence and basic competences in science and technology
- digital competence
- **Learning to Learn**
- social and civic competences
- sense of initiative and entrepreneurship
- cultural awareness and expression.

Of considerable significance was the inclusion of Learning to Learn as a key competence. Not only was Europe recognising Learning to Learn as a key lifelong learning performance indicator, it was also recognising it as a competence: something that could be measured.

It is important at this juncture to lay some common ground with regard to what is meant by competence in this context. It is also useful to state what it is not: it is not simply skills and knowledge. As in the *Sabre-tooth Curriculum* (Peddiwell, 1939), it is not surface learning; in other words, observable behavioural skills and acquisition of knowledge passed on from one generation to the next with no acknowledgement as to how the world has changed.

Competence has a broader meaning of skills and knowledge, one that moves our perception of competence from 'knowing that' or 'what we know' to describing the processes by which we create knowledge or 'how we know' (Organisation for Economic Cooperation and Development [OECD], 2005). If you refer to the definition of Learning to Learn on page 5, the reference to competence should assume greater significance and the sense of a holistic approach to learning is developed. In this context, the importance to lifelong learning (as decided by the European Council), is that the Learning to Learn competence is highly relevant for developing and updating job-related skills, which are constantly changing.

Effective Lifelong Learning Inventory

With the advent of key competences, the European Commission wanted to develop an instrument for testing Learning to Learn. How else can they monitor the value for money and effectiveness of developing policy, systems and processes? Four national instruments on Learning to Learn were considered useful to create a European instrument. One of these four instruments was the Effective Lifelong Learning Inventory (ELLI) developed by The University of Bristol (Deakin Crick, Broadfoot and Claxton, 2004). The ELLI project aimed to define and measure a person's orientation towards effective lifelong learning. Lifelong learning is understood in this context as lifelong and 'lifewide'. The concept of 'building learning power' that was introduced earlier contains seven dimensions[3]:

- Changing and learning
- Meaning making
- Curiosity
- Creativity
- Learning relationships
- Resilience
- Strategic awareness.

Skills across the curriculum

The powerful influence of the Bologna Declaration and the Lisbon Strategy becomes even more apparent when we recognise the impact we are experiencing. In England, for example, a key resulting document was the Gilbert Report (2006). This report presented a 2020 vision for personalising teaching and learning for children and young people aged 5–16. It made recommendations about what changes to the school system should be considered and ways to improve and sustain the rate of pupil progress, strategies to enhance teachers' skills and share best practice, and how to engage pupils and parents in the learning process. This document itself influenced ways in which flexibilities in the curriculum might support personalised learning, and Learning to Learn was mentioned in this context[4].

---

[3] These are developed further in Chapter 4.

[4] Further information is available in Chapter 2.

In 2008, curricula changed in England, Wales, Scotland and Northern Ireland, and skill sets were introduced to improve learner ability to play an increasingly active and effective part in the learning process. Different terms might be used across the curricula, but at their core they have the values and concepts underpinning Learning to Learn[5].

The last word

We often hear that we are living in the information age. This period could equally be called the age of Learning to Learn. Not very long ago, young people would learn skills they could use in their work throughout life. Today, in industrial countries, most people are doing jobs that did not exist when they were born and, on average, an individual can be expected to have up to 14 job changes in their working lives. Technological advances have meant reduced idea-to-market timescales – so that in 3–4 months of reading this sentence, technology we haven't even thought of yet will be available to purchase in shops or online! The most important skill determining a person's life pattern has already become the ability to learn new skills, take in new concepts, assess new situations and to deal with the unexpected. This will be increasingly true in the future: the indomitable ability is the ability to learn to learn.

References

Deakin Crick, R., Broadfoot, P. and Claxton, G. (2004) 'Developing an Effective Lifelong Learning Inventory: the ELLI Project', in *Assessment in Education*, 11, (3): pp. 247–272.

Education Council (2006) 'Recommendation of the European Parliament and the Council of 18 December 2006 on key competencies for lifelong learning', *Official Journal of the European Union*: 49 (10): ISSN: 1725-2555.

European Council (2000) *Presidency Conclusions, Lisbon European Council 23–24 March 2000*. Brussels, European Council.

Gilbert, C. (2006) *2020 Vision: Report of the Teaching and Learning in 2020 Review Group*. Nottingham: DfES. ISBN: 978-1-844788-62-0.

McGettrick, B. (2002) *Transforming School Ethos: Transforming Learning Citizenship Education in Action*. Paper presented at Bristol University Graduate School of Education.

OECD (2005) *The Definition and Selection of Key Competencies Executive Summary*. Web document: www.oecd.org/dataoecd/47/61/35070367.pdf (Accessed 30 October, 2008).

Reflective Activity

The purpose of this activity is to develop awareness of yourself and colleagues as learners.

1   What do you understand by the term 'effective learner'?

2   Share your current approach to learning with colleagues at a departmental/school meeting and identify the key features.

3   Is there a convergence in terms of a departmental/school approach to learning? Can you map the key features?

4   What do you think were the type and nature of key experiences you encountered that have shaped this thinking?

5   How would you describe/summarise the nature of the learning experiences you are framing for your learners?

6   Discuss with colleagues the extent to which you develop learners as learners and their process skills as opposed to delivering content. How does this approach change when teaching core physical education and examination of physical education?

7   How do you approach your own learning?

8   How do you and your colleagues currently embrace the skills curriculum? Is it perceived as something to cover, or something that will help learners become better learners?

---

[5] Please see Table 3: Summary of the seven dimensions of learning power, in Chapter 4.

Peddiwell, J. A. (1939) 'The Sabre-tooth Curriculum', in: Golby, M., Greenwald, J. and West. R. (eds) (1975). *Curriculum Design*. London: The Open University Press, London. ISBN: 978-0-856642-18-5.

Further Reading

Websites:

Association for Physical Education (afPE):
www.afpe.org.uk

Building Learning Power:
http://esd.escalate.ac.uk/downloads/1736.pdf

Centre for Research on Lifelong Learning: www.crll.org.uk

Deep and Surface Learning:
www.learningandteaching.info/learning/deepsurf.htm

Effective Life Long Learning Inventory (ELLI):
www.ellionline.co.uk

The Bologna Declaration 1999:
www.bologna-bergen2005.no/Docs/00Main_doc/990719
BOLOGNA_DECLARATION.PDF

The encyclopaedia of informal education:
www.infed.org/encyclopaedia.htm

The Lisbon Strategy:
http://en.wikipedia.org/wiki/Lisbon_Strategy
http://europa.eu/scadplus/glossary/lisbon_strategy_en.htm

Theory into practice (TIP) – major theories of learning:
http://tip.psychology.org

UK National Curricula homepages:
http://curriculum.qcda.gov.uk

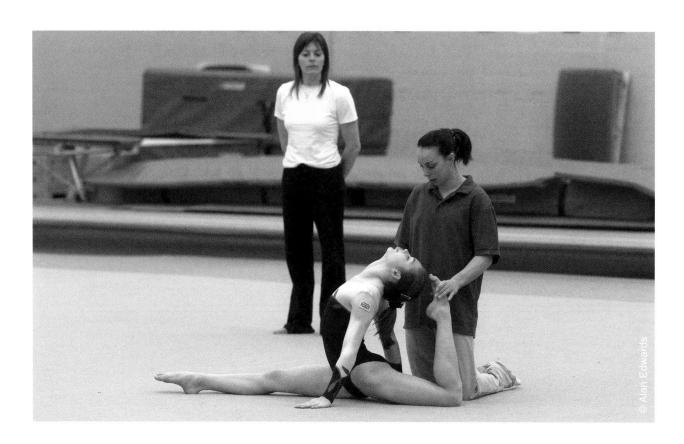

Chapter 2: Personalising Learning as a Context for Learning to Learn: Deep Learning

Purpose

The purpose of this chapter is to provide the bigger picture or the context for the concept of Learning to Learn. Personalising learning is explored as an approach to raising standards and as a whole-school philosophy. Learning to Learn is portrayed as an essential constituent of this approach.

Key Messages

- Personalising learning is an approach to learning that moves away from teacher-led, traditional interactive learning, and wholly puts the learner at the heart of the system.
- The approach involves giving due consideration to many interrelated areas; one of which focuses on developing learners to become better learners (Learning to Learn).
- Education is 'done with' learners, not 'done to' learners.
- Learners have choices of how to learn, when they learn (through flexible timetabling), where they learn and with whom.
- Learning how to learn is a foundation stone of personalising learning.

Introduction and Background

In the 1980s the mobile phone cost the same as a small vehicle (and often needed that same vehicle to transport it, such was its size). By 2002, global subscriptions to mobile phones passed the two-billion mark. With the advance in technology and clever marketing, the cost of owning a mobile phone reduced dramatically and demand for a product that offered opportunity for customisation increased. As such, the mobile phone industry was one of the first exponents of the mass customisation concept, a term introduced in business in 1987. What made this possible were two key interrelated developments to considering a product or products. The first was digitisation, which makes personalisation much easier. The second was modularisation. In the same way that Lego blocks could be chunked together, so too could the modular aspects of a mobile handset; from its casing colour, theme, polyphonic ringtones and wallpaper, to features such as digital camera, media player, text messaging and Bluetooth. The selection or preference for personalised phones has extended to accessories such as carry cases, earpieces and in-car chargers and holders.

Personalising a mobile phone has become a multi-billion-pound business worldwide, and shows no signs of slowing down. Today, mobile phone companies offer customisation or personalisation as the heart of their strategy for mobile phone growth. The customers' preferences drive what is produced and some companies are already offering a standard basic unit with opportunity for customers to select their own modular features, depending on needs and cost.

Similarly, in education and training there has been a growing awareness that a one-size-fits-all approach to school knowledge, curriculum design, timetables, organisation, support, teaching, learning and assessment is ill-adapted both to individuals' needs and to the requirements of employers and society. To move beyond what could generally be described as uniform mass provision, is to embrace a wider, more personalised approach to education and public services in general.

The rapid evolution of information and communication technologies (ICT), as well as learning sciences research into the functioning of the brain, has created a shift in emphasis from a teaching to a learning paradigm. This, in turn, has provided the opportunity for implementing a personalised learning approach.

This emerging emphasis on personalised learning is closely tied with the principles of helping all children achieve more, and is a rapidly developing central educational premise. This is true not just of England, but also the USA, Australia and New Zealand.

A personalised approach essentially promotes respect and consideration of learners' needs, allowing them to exercise choice about what and how they learn. Professor David Hargreaves (2005) prefers the term 'personalising learning' to 'personalised learning' because it suggests a process or a journey rather than a personalised-learning product.

What is Personalising Learning?

A shift towards personalising learning fundamentally means two considerations:

- How can we tailor learning to the needs, interests and aspirations of each individual?
- How can we break down barriers to learning and allow all learners to achieve their potential?

What is important to realise here, is that in responding to these prompts, schools/institutions are placing the learner at the core of their decision making, and decisions about strategy and ideas for action are focused on supporting learners in the process.

The term 'personalised learning' first entered the education arena in former Prime Minister Tony Blair's speech at the 2003 Labour Party Conference. At a North of England Education Conference in January 2004, the former Secretary of State for Education, David Milliband, emphasised that the government drive would be to make personalised learning universal. In 2006, the Gilbert Report supported a personalised learning approach, and in his acceptance speech in June the following year, former Prime Minister, Gordon Brown, stated: 'This personalised approach to learning is at the heart of the next stage of education reform'.

According to the former Department for Education and Skills (DfES), now the Department for Education, there are five key components of personalised learning as shown in Figure 2.1 (adapted from the former DfES standards website).

Figure 2.1 shows the five components of personalised learning and how they fit together. The components are interrelated and form a mutually supportive integrated whole. They offer a framework for implementation: a 'road map' for schools and teachers to utilise in their own context. Action and strategy employed by the school to respond to a shift towards personalised learning will therefore be locally determined. The Inner Core essentially focuses on classroom practice. This includes the integration of: curriculum; assessment; and learning and teaching (pedagogy). When these components are considered, planned and employed, with learners at the heart of the process, the learners become a central part of the education process rather than a product for whom education is something that is done to or happens to them.

The plethora of strategies that can be used will be decided by schools in terms of the professional attributes, knowledge and understanding, skills of the teachers and support staff, and the individual needs of the learner.

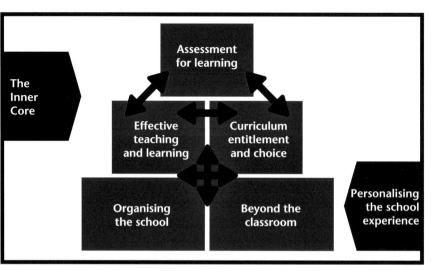

Figure 2.1: The five components of personalised learning

An overabundance of support materials has been produced through the National Strategy work and this is now manifesting in practice in the new curricula in England, Wales, Scotland and Northern Ireland (all implemented 2008).

Classroom practice is supported by a focus on how the school is arranged for personalised learning to occur (personalising the school experience). Personalisation demands a radical approach to school and class organisation based around student progress. Workforce reform is a key factor in promoting this component, as is the effective use of ICT. The diverse needs of learners are best met when teachers have a range of adults other than teachers working with them, and ICT to support this. ICT can permeate all of the building blocks in the diagram, enhancing creativity, extending learning opportunities and sustaining varied and challenging learning through a one-to-one, one-to-many or group-to-group arrangement.

Personalised learning also means the community, local institutions and social services that support schools to drive forward progress in the classroom. This requires coherence of a multi-layered, multi-agency approach and 'Parents for Learning' are seen as a key group in establishing this component. The Learning Outside the Classroom (LOtC) manifesto was another key driver in enriching personalisation, establishing, maintaining and raising standards.

The Nine Gateways to Personalising Learning

The DfES offered the five components of personalised learning as a framework for delivery. If we view personalised learning as an umbrella term, then it becomes easier to understand the logic of locally determined approaches within this framework. Constituent parts that form a personalised learning approach become apparent as part of a broader philosophy, helping to shape coherence and a way forward. To that end, in 2004 Professor Hargreaves worked with more than 200

school leaders to develop a further understanding of the constituent parts of a personalisation approach. It centred on what schools were already doing to embrace the notion of how to personalise learning. The result was the production of a framework made up of **nine learning gateways**. Subsequent work, conferences and meetings promoted an understanding of the complex relationships between the gateways and these were synthesised into what was termed the **four deeps** (see Figure 2.2 adapted from Hargreaves, 2006).

It is not the focus of this chapter to explore each of the four deeps (websites for further reading are provided at the end of the chapter), rather, to provide the context for Learning to Learn in terms of the personalising learning agenda. If we understand and are beginning to implement the paradigm shift from a focus on teaching, content and coverage, towards learning based around learner needs, then it is also incumbent to ask: how do we progress from a focus on learning to deep learning? The deep learning cluster outlined in Figure 2.2 includes Learner Voice (we have adapted this from Pupil Voice to indicate the notion of parallel learning processes – teachers are also learners first), Assessment for Learning (AfL) and Learning How to

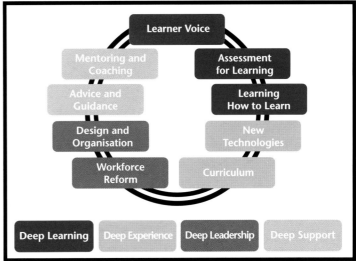

Figure 2.2: The nine gateways and the four deeps (adapted from Hargreaves, 2006)

Learn (LHTL). The relationship is depicted in Figure 2.3 in a diagram taken from the Gilbert Report (2006), although Pupil Voice is used where we prefer Learner Voice.

Deep learning

Interestingly, in each of the four case studies included in Chapter 5, the institutions integrate Learner Voice, AfL and Learning to Learn to advance the learning ethos of the establishments. None of the institutions have approached Learning to Learn as simply a programme to be implemented, and learners are viewed as an essential part of an integrated and complex process.

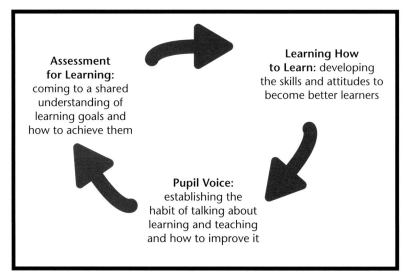

© Crown

Figure 2.3: The gateways to deep learning

Learner Voice – subjects or citizens?

The curricula provide wonderful opportunities for teachers (as learners) and learners to collaborate in designing and engaging in learning. This should not be a one-off, but an ongoing dialogue. The engagement of learners can move beyond simple 'involvement' and making decisions about the environment to a role that involves them designing curricula, having a choice about the range and content followed, and the learning and teaching methods employed. It is important to distinguish between learner wants and needs in this context, and to manage professional development strategically so that, for example, a department's five-year 'futures vision-provision' for their learners can be implemented effectively. The Christian Malford narrative in Chapter 5, where the learners hold the head teacher accountable for school development and achievement of targets, is a great example of learning conversations taking place between adults and young learners and promoting pupils or students as learning partners. Such situations allow learners the opportunity to influence decisions beyond the sometimes tokenistic school

councils where only the most articulate young people get a voice (which can sometimes be a barrier to democracy). Learner voice needs to be inclusive so a range of opportunities can be provided; from decisions about learning in lessons; to choices about activities followed; to decisions about school policy and school-development planning.

Assessment for Learning

The former Department for Children, Schools and Families (DCSF) launched its AfL Strategy in 2008, which ran until 2011. This is not a process promoted solely in English schools; rather, it is a worldwide phenomenon. What has developed is the notion that the responsibility for learning should be shared by the teacher and learner wherever possible. This shift views good teaching as being centred on the facilitation of pupil/student learning. The focus of attention is firmly upon the learner, and teacher activity is of value or interest only in respect of what it enables learners to achieve. This is occurring globally and across all subjects as the nature of teaching and learning changes.

The shift to a focus on the learner initially brought about an abundance of types of assessment that happen after learning has taken place. Information when gathered and recorded by the teacher is usually transformed into marks or grades. Performance is often compared with others and reviewed in the context of past learning. This overemphasis on Assessment **of** Learning has now shifted to an emphasis on Assessment **for** Learning. The resultant actions might differ globally, but the DCSF's 2008 AfL strategy centred on using assessment information to monitor and inform learners' progress. The use of information for learning on a day-to-day, periodic and transitional basis is essential for effective communication between learner and teacher.

Learning to Learn

AfL, then, could and should be a key part of a process to build learning power. An increasing number of schools are beginning to embrace Learning to Learn ideas. Several schools deliver Learning to Learn through discrete units of work. Others provide topic-based work and focused aspects of Learning to Learn are delivered across subjects. Schools are working with Guy Claxton's four Rs, Campaign for Learning's five Rs or Bristol University's seven dimensions as approaches[6]. Essentially, as outlined in Chapter 1, the vital concept is that learners' awareness of themselves as learners is promoted and the competencies, however framed (four, five or seven categories), can be learned and developed and, in turn, make a significant improvement to an individual's learning power. Deep learning is achieved when learners are able to assess learning principles of 'where am I now?' 'where am I targeting?' and 'how will I get there?', and combine these with the appropriate insightful skills of Learning to Learn. Learner Voice is promoted through the dialogue generated when engaging in learning tasks framed around AfL interacting with Learning to Learn ideas. This interrelationship serves to remind us that learning is a process and not something simply done to the learner.

Finally, in terms of the bigger picture and taking the next step, it is worth noting the ideas of Coimbatore Krishnarao Prahalad of the University of Michigan Ross School of Business, whose ideas centre on best practice and next practice. Best practice asks what is working. Prahalad (2004) suggested we focus on next practice and ask 'what could work more powerfully'? In that respect, the following question is a useful starting point: 'how can our next practice in these three areas facilitate deep learning?'[7]

Myths Exploded

When discussing the notion of personalising learning with colleagues, there are a number of myths that are often raised. For whatever reason, these myths tend to gather momentum, often because it is easier to make sense of things from what we already know and understand, rather than develop understanding through deep learning. Indeed, even the Teaching Learning and Research Programme (TLRP)/Economic and Social Research Council (ESRC) 2010 warned there is a danger that the discussion of personalised learning may lose its focus on learning and slip back into an over-simplified consideration of teaching provision and associated systems.

Myth 1: Personalising learning is the same as individual learning.

Personalising learning does not mean we leave learners to learn on their own, nor does it mean we have to create an individual learning programme or individual lesson plans for every learner. Collaborative and community learning can still be encouraged, although independent learning can complement this.

Myth 2: Personalising learning is the same as differentiation.

No it is not. Differentiation is obviously linked, but this is inevitably teacher-led even if differentiating by task. Differentiation, if it is learner-centred (in that there is an element of learner choice), becomes part of a personalising approach.

---

[6] See Chapters 3 and 4.

[7] The CD-ROM *Entering New Worlds: From Best Practice to Next Practice* authored by Andrew Frapwell is a useful resource supporting deep learning in physical education.

Myth 3: Personalising learning is a new theory of learning.

No. What is being advocated is an approach to thinking about learning and promoting opportunities for deeper learning. Schools have a responsibility to set the conditions for this based on learner needs. So an awareness of multiple intelligences and learning styles is also linked, but not, as Howard Gardner (who developed the notion of multiple intelligences) contends, as a tool to label pupils, but so that teachers can provide a range of learning experiences and opportunities to engage pupils emotionally, physically and intellectually.

Myth 4: Personalising learning is just 'old milk in new cartons'.

To truly personalise learning, there are huge implications for our practice. This means shifting the emphasis of everything we do to focus on the learners and their needs. The 2008 curricula in England, Wales, Scotland and Northern Ireland support this personalising learning approach and those who believe they can maintain their current practice or provision and simply replace old language with new language are seriously missing the point. There is a real opportunity here to transform our approach to improve learning and learners.

Reflective Activity

The purpose of this activity is to consider the coherence of your current personalising learning approach.

1   List the gateways you currently utilise.

2   How do the gateways currently complement each other?

3   In terms of the learning cluster, how do you currently promote deep learning?

4   How might you promote 'next' practice?

5   In what contexts do you encourage learning conversations (with learners, colleagues, or the wider community)?

6   How are or how might learner abilities be monitored in the three learning gateways of deep learning? Why is this important?

References

Sebba, J., Brown, N., Steward, S., Galton, M. and James, M. (2007) *An Investigation of Personalised Learning Approaches used by Schools*. Research Report No 843. Nottingham: DfES. ISBN: 978-1-844789-32-0.

Frapwell, A. (2007) *Entering New Worlds: From Best Practice to Next Practice*. (CD-ROM) Worcester: Tacklesport.

Gardner, H. (1983) *Frames of mind: The theory of multiple intelligences*. New York: Basic Books. ISBN: 978-0-465025-08-4.

Gilbert, C. (2006) *2020 Vision: Report of the Teaching and Learning in 2020 Review Group*. Nottingham: DfES. ISBN: 978-1-844788-62-0.

Hargreaves, D. (2005) *Personalising Learning 3: Learning to Learn and the New Technologies*. London: Specialist Schools Trust. ISBN: 978-1-905150-18-0.

Hargreaves, D. (2006). *Personalising Learning*. iNet/SSAT

National College for School Leadership (NCSL) (2005) *Leading Personalised Learning in Schools*. Web document: http://forms.ncsl.org.uk/media/1C9/81/leading-personalised-learning-in-schools.pdf

Prahalad, C. K. (2004) *The Fortune at the Bottom of the Pyramid: Eradicating Poverty through Profits*. University of Pennsylvania: Wharton School Publishing. ISBN: 978-0-137009-27-5.

Teaching Learning and Research Programme (TLRP) (2004) *Personalised Learning: A commentary by the teaching and learning research programme*. Swindon: Economic and Social Research Council (ESRC).

TLRP/ERSC (2010) *Professionalism and Pedagogy*. London General Teaching Council for England (GTCE) ISBN: 978-0-854738-97-7.

Further Reading

Websites:

Campaign for Learning:
www.campaign-for-learning.org.uk/cfl/index.asp

Economic and Social Research Council (ESRC):
www.esrc.ac.uk

Learning Outside the Classroom (LOtC): www.lotc.org.uk

Qualifications and Curriculum Development Agency (QCDA): www.qcda.gov.uk

Specialist Schools Academies Trust (SSAT):
www.ssatrust.org.uk/Pages/home.aspx

Department for Education website:
www.education.gov.uk/schools

The DfES standards website:
http://webarchive.nationalarchives.gov.uk/200801080006
49/http://www.standards.dfes.gov.uk/schemes2/phe/

Teaching and Learning Research Programme (TLRP):
www.tlrp.org/pub/index.html

Association for Physical Education (afPE):
http://www.afpe.org.uk/

Chapter 3: Finding Significance

Purpose

This chapter outlines the importance of **meaning making** in moving to an understanding of Learning to Learn concepts. Meaning making not only of research findings, individual and institutional narrative, but, also our own worlds. Common approaches in terms of taxonomy are summarised and identified from Guy Claxton's work, Campaign for Learning, and the Teaching, Learning and Research Project (TLRP). Recommendations are made for the reader, but the overriding messages are of context, readiness for change and change processes.

'There is nothing that is a more certain sign of insanity than doing the same thing over and over again and expecting a different result.'

Albert Einstein

Key Messages

- Harnessing the power of story.
- You can't really share meaning until you've shared context.
- Learning, unlearning and re-learning – tools and processes are synonymous.
- Research matters.

'Thou shalt not is soon forgotten, but once upon a time' will last forever.

Philip Pullman

The land of story

According to an old wives' tale, an idiot cannot sneeze. So when a grandmother telephones to ask if a newborn baby has sneezed, based solely on the fact that her mother had relayed the very same story, the power of story becomes apparent.

A belief is held in Germany that three sneezes before breakfast means you will receive a present during the day. Other countries have their own stories about sneezing and all have a powerful influence on behaviours. The same is true of other superstitions – how many colleagues or friends do you know who, having spilt salt, take a pinch of it to throw over their shoulder, or those who make a gesture or sign of some sort if they see a magpie?

Think also to nursery or primary school contexts. In order to help children make sense of this world we tell them stories; stories with meaning. A common story related to young children is 'The boy that cried wolf'; the message of which is, don't tell lies.

Once Upon a Time

'While algebraic and bureaucratic paradigms of thought can only simplify, story can complicate. While mathematics of human behaviour can only count, reduce and alienate, story can enrich, enliven, connect. What mathematics diminishes, story nurtures. What algebra renders invisible, story values. As mathematics standardises, so story makes unique.

'The signpost to the future points back toward the land of story, for it is over this horizon that further understanding is to be found.'

Dadds (1995, p.166)

An obvious analogy can also be drawn with education practices and behaviours, and this in itself is very worrying. Take, for example, the profession's use of attainment targets and level descriptors since the turn of the century. A whole industry has grown up around the use of attainment target level descriptors, including hierarchically dividing the level descriptors for foundation subjects into sub-levels, levelling individual pieces of work or activities, averaging levels given, and an obsession to convert every bit of progress a child makes

"Poor learners can become good learners."

into a number or grade. The profession has created a whole layer of assessment activity around attainment targets and level descriptors, yet the levels were never meant to be used this way. Not one piece of guidance from the Qualifications and Curriculum Development Agency (QCDA), the National Assessment Agency (NAA), the Office for Standards in Education (Ofsted) or government departments, has ever directed us towards these practices.

Were we aware of such guidance, but due to myths and stories that abounded, we failed to make sense of this guidance? Did senior leadership team requirements and our own circumstances create a more powerful context for meaning? The most worrying aspect is that in 2000 the Physical Education Association of the United Kingdom (PEA UK)[8] issued a statement that language such as Level 2 games or Level 4 dance 'should not be used'. In 2007, the QCDA's attainment target section of its National Curriculum in Action website issued the following statement for all subjects: 'Please note level descriptions are not designed to be used to "level" individual pieces of work'.

What this particular account highlights is the increasing power of story in influencing not just our everyday lives, but also the professional workplace. 'Coughs and sneezes spread diseases' is a saying that gives publicity to the fact that thoughtlessness helps spread not only the common cold but other diseases as well. The dilemma highlighted is that story sharing without an evidence base, without context or meaning, can spread misconceptions leading to poor or undisciplined professional practice.

In Chapter 5 we share people's stories or narratives and in Chapter 6 we share several isolated solutions to various challenges using Learning to Learn ideas in practice. It is important, therefore, that these chapters and information are not seen as blueprints to follow, rather, they highlight that we need to be acutely aware of two things: first, the term context and the schools context are major factors in

meaning making and, second, the narrative itself is considered in conjunction with several viewpoints, including other people's research and one's own personal experience. As such, this book seeks to provide a vehicle for a learning journey that goes some way to achieving these conditions. In this way it is hoped myths, old wives' tales or superstitions will not evolve to promote misunderstandings leading to poor, static and balkanised practice.

Meaning Making/Meaning Breaking

Crises of meaning

Many children of primary school age receive their first ever 'reality check' when they discover from their playground friends that Father Christmas or Santa Claus doesn't exist. This can be a big shock to firmly held beliefs and, as a result, children may well deny this message for a while and will often seek verification from parents or grandparents, who are often the people promoting this untruth in the first place. The obvious disappointment can be dramatic when parents reveal that Father Christmas is not a true figure.

The film The Da Vinci Code released in 2006 is another example. Based on an original book by American author, Dan Brown, it gave exposure to the unorthodox doctrine that Jesus had married Mary Magdalene, fathered children with her and therefore had a bloodline. This revelation brought uproar and condemnation from thousands of believers and several quarters, not least the Catholic Church. Scores of people refused to even contemplate or discuss the idea, passing it off as 'Hollywood claptrap'.

Whether a young person who believes in Father Christmas, or a head teacher or subject leader who believes we should frequently allocate a number or a grade to anything that moves – it is sometimes difficult to consider any contradictions to what gives our lives meaning. The whole process of challenging firmly held epistemological beliefs and practice can provoke a crisis of meaning.

[8] In 2006 PEA UK merged with the British Association of Advisors and Lecturers in Physical Education (baalpe) to form the Association for Physical Education (afPE).

Context

When observing election campaigns, all candidates can be very convincing and it is difficult to choose which political party is speaking the truth. For some, the decision might be down to individual personality, while, for others it might be down to which politics best suit their own context. Reality or truth for most people becomes that which is more relative or more appropriate to their own context. In other words, how relative something is to our own version of it. In recognising the importance of context there has been a move to contextual learning or 'learning outside the classroom' that is reality-based. In addition, the introduction of core tasks in England or rich tasks in Wales are an attempt to ensure physical education is contextual to the learner and learning. They are authentic contexts for performance.

According to Bruner (1996) the notion of folklore that arose when describing life in the Middle Ages has now become folk pedagogy in many areas of education. In challenging this **folk pedagogy** or falsehoods, 'self-lore' and context are required.

Meaning breaking

Many of us will have faced a crisis of meaning in life or work at some stage. As educators, our experiences are frequently the result of government, school or even departmental policy that has been imposed. If context is not explained, it is very difficult to make meaning, and even more difficult to support the implementation of initiatives at whatever school hierarchical level. More often than not, this lack of meaning can lead to authority being challenged, complete apathy or implementation disquiet. The important question is how, when our meaning falls apart or breaks, do we piece it together again? This has major implications not only for self-help, but for how continuing professional development (CPD) is organised and delivered, including a view of CPD going beyond just courses. Learners, including teachers, need to own their individual development and 'meaning investigations'. In

other words, they need to think for themselves otherwise a spoon-fed culture will evolve.

Learning, unlearning, relearning

Bruner (1996) believes it is essential that prior beliefs are taken into account when challenging practice or contradicting meaning, because any new material will have to '...compete with, replace or otherwise modify the folk theories that already guide both teachers and pupils.' Schratz and Walker (1995) suggest that in a period of multiplex social and cultural change, recognising prior learning may be exactly the wrong thing to do; it might be more important to recognise people's capacity to unlearn (and perhaps correspondingly our capacity to un-teach). Practical tips for teachers, resources produced by commercial companies (eg including prescriptive units of work) and instructing people how to do things, might be helpful for beginner or less confident teachers in the short term, but they need to be rapidly built on in coherent, progressive programmes of professional development in the medium and longer term. Central to such programmes should be opportunities for teachers to re-evaluate their beliefs about learning, the way they structure tasks and their conceptions of classroom roles and relationships. Practical-based inquiry or **action research** has a crucial part to play in this. However, this opens up teacher practice to critical scrutiny, collaboration and a readiness to take responsibility for decisions, action and consequences, so there is an element of risk-taking that some institutions appear unwilling to embrace for fear of failure. To make such change easier, structures and cultures need to be created that provide staff with the confidence to innovate, cyclical support processes and the ability to learn from practice. The current curricula in the UK afford this flexibility and a freedom to innovate, but it will not happen if the willingness of institutions and individual learners to unlearn is absent, or if the context, as described, is deficient.

"Encourage innovation."

This process could be compared to Lewin's (1952) unfreeze-change-refreeze process. The unfreeze phase involves diagnosis: assessing the situation and prescribing an appropriate change strategy. The change phase is implementing change strategy through enhanced collaboration and cooperation. The refreeze phase is addressing unanticipated problems and side effects, and the evaluation of the effectiveness of change strategy (Kreitner, 1995). When compared to institutional change, it is no coincidence that the implementation of the secondary curriculum in England (QCA, 2007) has been centred on this change process or **disciplined innovation**. It is no coincidence, either, that if we look at this process and the learning skills required for it to happen, we are describing the Assessment for Learning (AfL) process and relating the principles and practice of Learning to Learn.

Relevance

Learning to Learn cannot, therefore, just simply be seen as a programme to be employed, a skill set or a tool that will provide solutions to problems. It also has to be viewed as a process of implementing change with all learners (including teachers) so that change is relevant to the learner context, evidence-based and appears meaningful. This will be an evolving process and goes beyond us as authors or any reformer for that matter, thinking that we only need to explain Learning to Learn for it to be accepted or understood.

Research Matters

Learning How to Learn: The Teaching and Learning Research Programme (TLRP)

The TLRP has six aims based around **Learning, Outcomes, Lifecourse, Enrichment, Expertise** and **Improvement**. The TLRP was inaugurated to develop the UK knowledge base

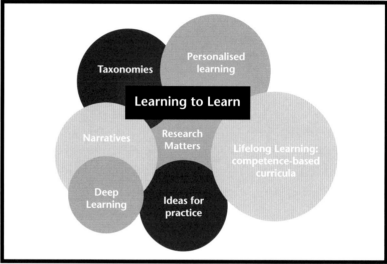

Figure 3.1: Diagram to highlight the areas considered in this book. How do we each make meaning from this?

on teaching and learning and to ensure this is applied in practice and policy. Learning How to Learn in Classrooms, Schools and Networks (LHTL) was researched over a four-year period (2001–2005) and was one of numerous research projects that TLRP managed. The work on this project was forged by four main researchers: Professor Mary James of the Institute of Education, University of London; Professor Robert McCormick of the Open University; Dr Bethan Marshall of King's College London; and Dr David Pedder from Cambridge University, but also involved other researchers from these universities. The research was conducted in 17 secondary, 21 primary and two infant schools from five local authorities and one virtual education action zone. They were chosen to provide a balance of urban and rural, large and small, and mono- and multi-ethnic schools.

The work focused on three areas:

* The practices likely to promote LHTL and how they overlap with, and build upon, those associated with AfL.

- Scaling up much of the small-scale research and evidence for the effectiveness of AfL.
- Development of innovative LHTL practices linked to AfL.

AfL is an assessment process that aims to encourage learners to assume greater responsibility (peer and self-assessment) for their progress and to become proactive in their learning. As well as a focus on questioning and feedback, learners are helped to understand the success criteria on which tasks are assessed and the thinking underpinning these criteria. Learners become partners in the learning process; they are aware of their starting point, the targets they are seeking to achieve, and, more importantly, they have strategies for getting there or closing the gap. The LHTL initiative was designed to build on this practice.

What was interesting about the design of the research was that it sought to develop project ideas to schools through an integrated professional development approach. This involved In Service Education and Training (INSET) sessions, optional sessions, base lining, critical friend time, meetings for school and local authority coordinators, and the use of a website for the exchange of ideas and materials. On the research side, evidence was collated to describe and explain the different patterns of implementation and impact. Questionnaires were developed to collect quantitative data on teachers' and pupils' beliefs about learning, staff values and reported practices concerning classroom assessment, professional learning, school leadership and management, and the use of electronic tools. This methodology promoted context, recognised individual's worlds and supported meaning breaking and meaning making.

Table 1: Summary of Learning How to Learn research findings[9]			
Whole School Approach	**Implementation – Teachers and Learning**	**Learners**	**Networking**
Opportunity and time to collaboratively evaluate practice was important to promote independent learning practices.	Most teachers were implementing the procedures of AfL to the letter, such as sharing assessment criteria with learners and accommodating peer or self-assessment sessions.	Primary learners saw little connection between particular school learning practices and the extent to which they felt involved and took initiative in their learning.	Teachers and schools made very little use of technology to communicate.
School policy initiatives and working groups influenced change.	Only 20% of teachers, however, implemented AfL in a way that enabled learners to become more independent as learners, a defining characteristic of LHTL.	Secondary learners saw learning practices and taking initiative in their learning as related, although their sense of active involvement in their learning declined.	Communications rarely involved the exchange of ideas about professional practice.

[9] Adapted from Teaching and Learning Research Briefing, July 2006

Table 1: Summary of Learning How to Learn research findings[9] (Continued)			
Whole School Approach	**Implementation – Teachers and Learning**	**Learners**	**Networking**
An inclusive school culture encouraging independent learning and ownership was vital. Ideas flowed from the bottom up as well as from the top down.	The above 20% of teachers shared certain characteristics, including: • a strong belief in the importance of their responsibility in promoting learner autonomy • an aptitude to reassess their practice when things went wrong rather than blaming external factors like exams or learners' abilities • an ability to communicate commitment to, and confidence in, the values of independent learning to their learners who, in turn, adopted them.		Large schools were complex networks in themselves, making it equally difficult to share knowledge within the school as it was between schools.
The support of school leaders was essential.	For 80% of teachers, there was a gap between what they valued and what they practised in the classroom, although the gap narrowed following intervention. Most felt constrained to put more emphasis on performance targets than they wished.		Analysing the networks available offers a way to exploit these valuable resources.

Conclusion

1   The AfL programme had frequently been implemented as a set of instructions handed down to teachers so the notion of independent learning had been overlooked. Some project schools achieved notable success in creating cultures of professional reflection and inquiry, which supported teachers in promoting independent learning in pupils.

2   LHTL is highly contextualised and cannot easily be separated from learning 'something'. It is not profitable to plan, teach or assess LHTL separately from planning, teaching or assessing learning in a specific subject.

3   Effective change is only likely to be achieved if individuals and organisations go beyond the implementation of surface procedures and engage with deeper principles of learning and teaching.

4   Teachers need the intellectual resources to 'know what to do when they don't know what to do'.

Of particular note is conclusion point 2 of Table 1. Several schools have implemented a programme of Learning to Learn that is distinct from specific subjects. This is not to say that learner independence has not been achieved, rather, it is more likely if Learning to Learn is seen as an integrative part of a coherent whole. This draws parallels with the approach in schools to the **knowledge and understanding of fitness and health** aspect of the National Curriculum (Department for Education and Employment [DfEE] Qualifications and Curriculum Development Authority [QCDA] 1999), in England. Ofsted (2005) reported that while discrete units of work promoting fitness and health in schools were followed, the knowledge was not, however, applied as integral to the various areas of activities. This issue was further compounded with the QCDA (2007) curriculum focus that learners should make informed decisions about healthy active lifestyles. Learners are required to make lifestyle changes and this engagement goes beyond simply knowing and understanding.

The Learning to Learn project: Campaign for Learning

Campaign for Learning started out as the Royal Society for the Encouragement of Arts, Manufacturers and Commerce (RSA) and became an independent charity in November 1997. The Society was created with the sole purpose of championing lifelong learning. The Learning to Learn project is split into two areas: Learning to Learn in schools and Learning to Learn in further education (FE).

Learning to Learn in schools

The former Department for Children, Schools and Families (DCSF) and the Innovation Unit supported the RSA work; much of which has influenced the direction of the secondary curriculum and is referred to in case studies on the QCDA website. The project demonstrated a positive impact on SATs results (abandoned at Key Stage 3 since 2009), motivation, attendance and behaviour, as well as on **soft skills.**

Learning to Learn in FE

The Learning to Learn in FE project is in its infancy, but opportunity to investigate the impact of Learning to Learn approaches in FE delivery and track progress of young people taught through these approaches in schools has been afforded.

The RSA characterised Learning to Learn as a learner awareness of:

- how to recognise their preferred learning and learning strengths
- how to self-motivate and develop the confidence to succeed
- the importance of such things as water, nutrition, sleep and a positive environment for learning
- some of the specific strategies to improve, for example, memory or making sense of complex information
- some of the habits to develop, such as reflecting on learning so as to improve next time.

"Lifelong learning is what we should all aspire to: lifelong learning is just as it says on the tin!"

Table 2: Summary of Learning to Learn project findings					
Learners	**Teachers and Teaching**	**Schools**	**Wider Community**	**Impact of Information and Communication Technology (ICT)**	**Participant Understanding of Learning to Learn**
Learners:	**Teachers:**				
• were overwhelmingly positive about Learning to Learn, motivated to learn and more aware of learning as a process	• valued the professional autonomy that the enquiry-based approach to action research afforded	The culture and structures of some schools fit better with the implementation of Learning to Learn.	Four schools focused their research explicitly on innovations for consulting and involving parents' interaction and involvement related to learning.	ICT was integral to the research approach.	Learning to Learn is not simply a set of activities or techniques that can be implemented in schools, rather, it is a range of interlocking methods and approaches that can be successful in supporting the development of effective learning habits and dispositions.
• developed a vocabulary for talking about learning and provided evidence of knowledge and understanding of their own learning	• were consistently positive about involvement in the Learning to Learn project and expressed increased motivation for their work	The success of Learning to Learn in schools has depended on the enthusiasm and commitment of key individuals, although these people are not necessarily in typical school-leadership roles.	Learning to Learn approaches have improved relationships and communication about learning between school and home.	It was the focus of a number of school-based investigations where it was found to contribute to effective teaching and learning.	An approach based on collaborative professional enquiry into Learning to Learn through the use of practical classroom strategies was clearly supportive of such development.

Learners	Teachers and Teaching	Schools	Wider Community	Impact of Information and Communication Technology (ICT)	Participant Understanding of Learning to Learn
Learners:	**Teachers:**				
• were skilful in the way they approached learning across different contexts	• adopted Learning to Learn approaches, which have allowed teachers the capacity to manage change effectively, finding new approaches and policy developments from a critical and professional standpoint.	In some schools Learning to Learn has provided a set of practices that has encouraged certain types of leadership, CPD and development processes for all staff.		ICT can support pupils' reflections on learning as they develop their understanding and learning capabilities.	
• had positive dispositions to learning and were more likely to be found where a school-wide approach to Learning to Learn was adopted.					

Taxonomies

> '"Learnacy" is more important than literacy and numeracy.'
>
> Professor Guy Claxton

The four Rs

Professor Guy Claxton has been debating, researching and writing about life, learning and thinking for over 30 years. He has published numerous papers and books that have influenced thinking about curricula around the world. His more recent research at the University of Bristol led to an association with the Teaching and Learning Organisation (TLO) to promote the concept of Building Learning Power (BLP), which was published as a book in 2002. BLP is classified under four headings or, as Claxton refers to them, **four major learning muscles**:

- **Resilience:** 'Being ready, willing and able to lock on to learning'. Being able to stick with difficulty and cope with feelings such as fear and frustration.
- **Resourcefulness:** 'Being ready, willing and able to learn in different ways'. Having a variety of learning strategies and knowing when to use them.
- **Reflection:** 'Being ready, willing and able to become more strategic about learning'. Getting to know our own strengths and weaknesses.
- **Relationships:** 'Being ready, willing and able to learn alone and with others'.

Underpinning this approach is the idea that teachers need to become **learning coaches** who can raise learner motivation, feed back, stretch and encourage and support them in reaching their goals. What he proposed, which is evident in much of the UK's curricula, was a **learning curriculum** that would shadow curriculum content at every stage. In addition, teachers need to adopt an approach of co-learner, where they feel comfortable to say, for example: 'I don't know the answer, let's work it out together'. In this way, Claxton suggests schools and universities can become very powerful learning places.

The five Rs

The Campaign for Learning project, supported by Newcastle University, has been researching Learning to Learn since 2000. The taxonomy that was developed from this work was referred to as the **five Rs:**

- **Resilience:** characterised by persistence, positivity, involvement, practice.
- **Resourcefulness:** showing initiative, learning differently, asking questions, taking risks.
- **Responsibility:** making moral choices, self-management, planning ahead, helping others.
- **Reasoning**: finding distinctions, considering evidence, choosing tools, taking time.
- **Reflection:** showing curiosity, valuing objectivity, adopting perspectives, using experience.

The seven dimensions

The research that led to the development of Claxton's four Rs was developed further by the University of Bristol. Synthesis of teacher stories and quantitative data resulted in the creation of the seven dimensions of learning power. The Effective Lifelong Learning Inventory (ELLI) project as it is known, began in 2002. It was funded by the Lifelong Learning Foundation and initiated by Professors Patricia Broadfoot and Guy Claxton.

ELLI learning profiles and training programmes are now available through Cambridge Education, while an ongoing research programme is being developed at the University of Bristol consisting of three parts:

- **Research and development projects**: local, research and learning partnerships.
- **Data development:** ongoing analysis of the data collected by ELLI online.

- **Research projects**: plans include a project exploring learning power and values, and a project exploring the 'ecology of learning' in a schooling system.

The seven dimensions are considered in further detail in Chapter 4.

What is clear from the research is that there is no 'one size fits all' with Learning to Learn. The action research undertaken by the various projects' teachers and learners, supported by university researchers, has generated a process of enquiry which is increasingly being recognised as a major factor in ensuring Learning to Learn becomes an embedded and enhancing practice in learner success stories. It appears that this continuing culture of contextual enquiry, self-awareness, reflective practice and meaning breaking/meaning making is the key, not only to creating Learning to Learn schools, but also to producing competent and confident lifelong learners.

Reflective Activity

The purpose of this activity is to raise awareness of your own values and context, and develop your own 'self-lore': your personal story.

1   What are your values or beliefs about education? What are you preparing learners for?

2   How do you currently keep abreast of the research into teaching and learning?

3   How do you currently seek evidence about the effectiveness of your own teaching and learning?

4   To what extent are AfL practices embedded in your practice? Are these teacher-directed AfL practices, or are learners independent in terms of the processes followed?

5   How do you currently embrace change? If your practices are challenged by a course you have attended, or something you have read, how do you respond?

6   Consider carrying out a departmental collaborative enquiry as a pilot for your institution.

References

Bruner, J. (1996) *The Culture of Education*. Cambridge MA: Harvard University Press. ISBN: 978-0-674179-53-0.

Claxton, G. L. (2002) *Building Learning Power: helping young people become better learners*. Bristol: Teaching and Learning Organisation Ltd. ISBN: 978-1-9012194-3-2.

Kreitner, R. (1995) *Management*. Chicago: Houghton Mifflin Company. ISBN: 978-0-395710-46-3.

Lewin, K. (1952). Discussed in: Goodstein, L. D. and Warner Burke, W. 'Creating successful organisation change'. *Organisation Dynamics*, 19, pp. 4–17.

TLRP/ESRC (2006) Teaching and Learning Research Briefing. No. 17, July 2006. London: TLRP

Schratz, M. and Walker, R. (1995) *Research as Social Change: New Opportunities for Qualitative Research*. London: Routledge. ISBN: 978-0-415118-69-7.

Further Reading

Websites:

Alite: www.alite.co.uk/index.php

Lifelong Learning Foundation: www.lifelonglearnresearch.co.uk/

TLRP – Publications as a result of the LHTL project: www.tlrp.org/users/cs2.html

Campaign for Learning: www.campaign-for-learning.org.uk/cfl/index.asp

Qualifications and Curriculum Development Agency (QCDA): www.qcda.gov.uk/

Chapter 4: Background to the Seven Dimensions

Purpose

This chapter highlights the importance of learning power and the responsibility to harness and nurture this ability in all learners. The background to the Effective Lifelong Learning Inventory (ELLI) seven dimensions are outlined, and the research and inventory for measuring the dimensions is explored in the context of moments in time and the need to develop a social conscience.

Key Messages

- An approach to building learning power, whichever taxonomy is used, should be a whole-school philosophy.
- There are readiness factors that should be in place before implementing Learning to Learn concepts.
- We have a responsibility to build learning power with all learners.
- Learning is transitory – we can only ever measure moments in time.
- Learning is learnable.
- A social conscience for learners and their learning should be fostered.

Learning Power and Responsibility

There is a growing body of research in the area of Learning to Learn. It is not of huge importance which taxonomy is utilised, as the concepts underpinning the field are the same. The common purpose is that we are providing for the development of learners as lifelong learners. What is essential, is a belief in the value of the Learning to Learn concept and an understanding that there are certain readiness factors that form the foundations for learner development within and beyond the curriculum. It is possible to make small changes to individual practice and these changes can reap success, but in order to gain maximum impact, Learning to Learn is best approached as a whole-school philosophy.

The list below is a summary of the whole-school readiness checklist we believe should be in place:

- A mentoring and coaching culture exists with an emphasis on support, solutions and standards.
- Learning and the learners should already be a focus when personalising curriculum provision, assessment strategy and effective pedagogy throughout the school.
- Effective tracking and recording systems and processes are in place as a means of reflecting on progress. These are integral to practice.
- Emphasis in assessment is on **improving** rather than **proving.**
- There is visionary leadership both at senior team and subject-leader level. Subject leaders are confident in leading and managing change.
- There is a disciplined innovation culture and space to take risks.

In this chapter, the ELLI seven dimensions have been chosen to explain the Learning to Learn concepts and the examination of their feasible roles within physical education and the whole school. The principles and concepts involved permeate the various taxonomies that are promoted in schools nationally, allowing flexibility and choice as to which taxonomy best fits the strategic needs of the school or institution.

We selected the seven dimensions as a particular focus as these are the areas in which we have most experience and they are uncomplicated when used in a physical education context. They are based on practical research carried out at the University of Bristol, which has led to online support resources, including a useful inventory for monitoring and reflecting on learner progress.

'With great power comes great responsibility'

This famous quote highlights the importance of Learning to Learn as a concept. The most popular source of this quote is taken from a conversation between the fictional characters of Uncle Ben and Peter Parker (Spiderman). Ben is trying to convince Peter of his responsibilities in life to

"Help your learners to develop coping mechanisms for when they encounter failure or perceived failure."

himself and others. He knows Peter has great potential; nevertheless, even he is surprised at how much that potential exceeds all expectations.

We can draw an analogy to education by comparing the learning power and the learning potential of learners we are responsible for. Until recently, learning power has been lying dormant, unrecognised and the possibilities left unexplored. This learning power can promote confidence in learners and their learning, can instil in learners a belief that they can continue to grow with or without help and can enable learners to develop coping strategies and skills for life and the challenges that life brings. It is truly influential. We have a responsibility to develop this learning power to broaden learners' personal horizons and steer away from the spoon-feeding culture that has emerged. As educators, perhaps we are guilty of doing too much to help learners when they could be doing more for themselves.

The learning dynamic

Consider your own successes and failures. What is your template for strategic action to ensure success? Do you address problems and discover solutions by continuously finding new ways of working? Do you know where to source relevant and helpful information? Do you know where to source inspiration? Do you use your own strategies? Have you failed in a task or failed to persevere in a task because you couldn't find a solution, couldn't change your working patterns, didn't know what to do, or who to go to or because you just weren't motivated? Using the example of exercise, as a nation, we have generally been poor at engaging in healthy active lifestyles. Too often we discontinue exercise because of the smallest inhibitor or barrier. The biggest inhibitor to engaging in physical activity is changing our lifestyle. We feel incapable of making changes to our lifestyle because we have learned to behave in a certain way and we make excuses, including the most common: insufficient time. This inability to adapt our lifestyle to incorporate exercise highlights an inability to **unlearn** and **re-learn** (see Chapter 3).

However, there are other instances of learning engagement and coping with failure that highlight a different approach or a different motivation; for example, a desire to succeed at all costs is often evident in adults who take the driving test. Those failing their test do not usually give up; they demonstrate perseverance by retaking the test and ensuring success. The motivation to achieve the goal of driving is often due to necessity and sometimes to feed the need of conforming to a society that values the car. The learning dynamic demonstrated in these two examples highlights a learning quandary; one that we need to understand and address. Learning and changing processes, which are presented in an irresistible, meaningful and relevant form, should provide a better motive for learners to engage in learning than: external pressures and targets (such as 'because it's on the syllabus specification'); external grades or numbers. Learning to Learn can promote an engagement with learning hitherto unknown.

Our ability to learn continuously changes. We all learn better in some contexts, at different times, stages and in different ways during a learning career. Learners who are aware of this ability can become more effective learners. Knowledge of starting points, progress towards targets, knowing how to establish and maintain learning momentum and knowledge of developing coping mechanisms when learning is stuck are all characteristics of being an effective learner. Understanding that learning is about moments in time and is dependent or related to numerous variables at any particular time is also to understand that there is no such thing as a poor learner. Learning and one's ability to learn at a particular moment in time is not something that is fixed; it is transitory. Only by acknowledging this can we help implement learner change. This is a key aspect of Learning to Learn in practice – the belief that learning is learnable.

The Seven Dimensions

Deakin Crick (2006) reported that following dialogue between Professors Patricia Broadfoot and Guy Claxton, and the trustees of the Lifelong Learning Foundation, a research project to develop and test an instrument for identifying an individual's capacity for lifelong learning was initiated. This was trialled with pupils across a range of ages and subjects, and resulted in seven dimensions of learning power being synthesised; providing a frame for the principles of Learning to Learn. Employing this approach and framework appeared to facilitate differentiation between efficacious, engaged and energised learners and passive, dependent and fragile learners (Deakin Crick, 2006). They are clearly laid out, easy to follow and user friendly.

The ELLI project was undertaken in the belief that a person's engagement with any particular learning opportunity was the result of a complex mix of learner dispositions, such as values, attitude, beliefs, social and life experiences. The second phase of the project explored how learning power related to other elements of learning, such as emotional climate and learner achievement. Training materials were subsequently produced and ELLI has now become more widely available.

The following is a descriptive list of the seven dimensions:

1 **Changing and learning:** a sense of changing and growing as a learner.

2 **Critical curiosity:** an inclination to ask questions, get below the surface of things and come to one's own conclusions.

3 **Meaning making:** making meaning personally meaningful by making connections between what is learned and what is already known.

4 **Creativity:** risk taking, playfulness, lateral thinking, and using imagination and intuition in learning.

5 **Learning relationships:** the ability to learn dependently, independently and interdependently.

6 **Strategic awareness:** being aware and actively managing one's own learning feelings, processes and strategies.

7 **Resilience:** the tenacity to persist in the face of confusion, the unknown and failure.

© Mark Bullimore

"Encourage pupils to work together to find solutions and use you only when required."

The following table provides a working description of each dimension and its polar opposite. The definitions are adapted from Deakin Crick (2006) and applied to a physical education context.

Table 3: Summary of the seven dimensions					
Dimension	**Description**	**Characteristics** **Learners:**	**Links to Physical Education**	**Polar Opposite**	**Links to Physical Education – Polar Opposite**
Changing and learning	• A sense of changing and growing as a learner.	• know that learning is learnable • feel good about the capacity to learn • expect to change over time • celebrate their own learning.	• Learners show a desire to improve • Learners show commitment to physical education and school sport.	Being stuck or static: • Low self-efficacy. • Views challenging situations as barriers to learning rather than opportunities.	• Learners are unaware of their strengths in physical education and unable to talk about progress they have made in specific activities. • Learners have limited evaluative skills.
Critical curiosity	• An inclination to ask questions, get below the surface of things and come to one's own conclusions.	• desire to delve deeper and find out what is going on • question and do not accept things at face value • want to know how, why, what and where • enjoy finding out.	• Learners think about what they are doing and make appropriate decisions. • Learners know and understand what they are trying to achieve.	Passivity: • Learners are more likely to accept what they are told uncritically. • Learners are less thoughtful and less likely to engage spontaneously in active exploration and exploratory discussion.	• Learners are unlikely to question the value of what they are doing. • Learners are less likely to surprise you with their response; for example, when composing a phrase or sequence in dance.

		Table 3: Summary of the seven dimensions (Continued)			
Dimension	**Description**	**Characteristics** **Learners:**	**Links to Physical Education**	**Polar Opposite**	**Links to Physical Education – Polar Opposite**
Meaning making	• Makes learning personally meaningful by making connections between what is learned and what is already known. • Maps new information to what is already known.	• make connections between subjects • love learning about what really matters to them • draw on their experiences in learning as well as the experiences of learning in the community and at home.	Coherence: • Learners are able to connect a range of physical education curriculum processes, concepts and content as opposed to engaging in separate sports • Learners view traditional curriculum time and out-of-school hours learning as a coherent offer • Learners are able to understand the value of physical education, per se • Learners link learning in other subjects (eg science with health-related exercise) • Learners can see the value in learning physical education has to their community sport work.	Fragmentation: • More likely to approach learning in a piecemeal way and to respond to situations as isolated learning with little or no reflection. • Information gained is compartmentalised	• Unable to see the link between physical education and other subjects such as science or mathematics. • View physical education and community activities as completely different entities.

Table 3: Summary of the seven dimensions (Continued)					
Dimension	**Description**	**Characteristics** **Learners:**	**Links to Physical Education**	**Polar Opposite**	**Links to Physical Education – Polar Opposite**
Creativity	• Takes risks in learning, playfulness, lateral thinking and using imagination and intuition in learning.	• enjoy playing with ideas and possibilities • trust their intuition and follow their hunches • use imagination in learning • enjoy being challenged and stretched.	Confident and imaginative: • Learners enjoy creating gymnastic sequences, dance composition or deciding tactics in games • Responses show imagination and may look very different to the responses of others.	Rule-boundness: • Learners tend to be unimaginative. They prefer clear-cut information and tried and tested ways of approaching things and they feel safer when they know how they are meant to proceed. • Function well in routine problem solving with clear-cut answers, but are less able when originality is required.	• Learners might be achieving effectively in a range of physical activities but responses lack imagination. • Happy to engage in activities they are comfortable with and follow rules, but reluctant to develop their own ideas.
Learning relationships	• Able to learn with and from other people, and to learn on their own.	• enjoy sharing thoughts and ideas with people • enjoy learning with and from other people • enjoy learning on their own • know how to help others learn.	Effective participants: • Learners enjoy the social aspects of learning in physical education and learn well in groups or as individuals • Learners are effective participants and able to take on a number of roles such as officiator, coach, leader and performer/learner • Learners can follow instructions and share ideas.	Isolation or dependence: • More likely to be stuck either in their over-dependency on others for reassurance or guidance, or in their lack of engagement with other people.	• Not particularly effective learners when in groups for any physical education activity. • Happy to sit back and let others suggest ideas and take on roles. • More likely to follow other people's responses when asked to problem solve.

Dimension	Description	Characteristics Learners:	Links to Physical Education	Polar Opposite	Links to Physical Education – Polar Opposite
Strategic awareness	• Being aware and actively managing own learning feelings, processes and strategies. • Knowing how to learn.	• manage own feelings of learning • plan learning carefully • think about thinking and learning • are aware of self as a learner; know what they like and dislike • are able to estimate how long a task will take.	Self-managers: • Learners enjoy the cognitive learning domain and think strategically when making appropriate decisions. • Learners have the control and skills needed and apply these to a variety of contexts • Learners develop coping strategies for winning, losing and confrontation • Learners understand that physical education and school sport is part of a healthy active lifestyle, and participate in a range of activities.	Passive, blinkered: • Less self-aware and likely to confuse self-awareness with self-consciousness. • Unlikely to be able to explain rationale for decisions made. Tend not to reflect and learn from their thought processes and experiences. • May engage in tasks without much planning or forethought. • Participates in a range of activities without any real reflection.	• Unable to explain the appropriateness of responses to tasks (eg devising routines or deciding on tactics).
Resilience	• The tenacity to persist in the face of confusion, not knowing and failure.	• know that making mistakes is a natural part of learning • are not afraid to have a go • tend to keep going at a task until it is completed • maintain their own pace and know they will get there in the end • understand that struggling is an important part of learning.	Stickability/ Bouncebackability • Learners persevere at new activities or skills they are working on, even when difficult. • Learners understand how to develop physical and mental capacity • Learners develop stamina, suppleness and strength and maintain a level of physical fitness and well-beings • Learners have a desire to improve and achieve.	Dependence and fragility: • Can go off task when stuck or after a mistake. • Avoid risk taking and unable to persevere on tasks, preferring to seek out less challenging situations. • Dependent on other people and external structures for emotional support. • Passive receivers of knowledge.	• Likely to give up easily when a new task is introduced; for example, if they are initially unsuccessful at a new skill in a game setting they will not persevere. • They are not willing to take risks and if asked to come up with a composition, a very safe performance will ensue.

Capturing Moments in Time

A proclivity in education is to concern ourselves with how something can be assessed and therefore how progress can be measured. This natural tendency inevitably leads teachers to ask if learning power can be assessed. Of vital importance at this juncture is our understanding of not only the concept of Learning to Learn, but also our understanding of the purposes of assessment, what is actually being quantified and how this is interpreted and used for future learning and teaching.

The Learning to Learn and assessment dynamic

If we reflect on the broad definitions of learning and Learning to Learn outlined in Chapter 1, what becomes apparent is that through Learning to Learn we can build learning power. This, in turn, allows learners to engage more effectively with the subject matter. Current research suggests there is a strong association, as opposed to a causal link, between improved learning power and learner progress and standards. Improved learning power, therefore, can be measured indirectly by improved progress in physical education, or by higher standards in physical education as measured against national benchmarks.

Accordingly, Learning to Learn and developing an individual's learning power should not be viewed as a programme, subject or examination; rather, it is a way of focusing on becoming better at learning. To formally assess Learning to Learn in this way would be to view it as something it is not intended to be. League tables and the perceived requirement to frequently collate data have, unfortunately, contributed to a mentality that seeks to prove assessment and learning have taken place, yet only serves to isolate these two elements. In these situations, data is used to analyse progress and standards, and, more often than not, only serves to highlight where pupils have made less progress than expected. In physical education, for example, this might draw attention to less progress in accurately replicating actions contrasted to greater progress in learning to outwit opponents. Progress data

will not highlight the fact that this might be associated with poor learner attitudes, poor framing of the content or learner deficiency in learning relationships or creativity, for example.

As described, the seven dimensions of Learning to Learn can therefore be used to impact on progress and standards, but learning can also be framed so as to impact on the seven dimensions: it is a mutually advantageous relationship.

Addressing the assessment conundrum

Having devised an instrument to measure the seven dimensions, the dilemma continues as to how assessment can be effectively employed as integral to a teaching and learning process, and how resulting data may be used to make informed decisions about its future development. In context, progress in learning and Learning to Learn is not linear and can vary over time. This is why too frequent testing or grading can often produce variable results. Progress is dependent on a range of factors and is often a product of the experiences a learner is going through at that moment in time. It is dependent on the learner's personal story and the context for the story. In the long term, while we would expect data surrounding school performance to demonstrate an upward trend, in the short term, learning processes and Learning to Learn dimensions do not follow the same pattern. The danger is that in our efforts to increase progress and attainment, we lose sight of the very essence of effective learning itself and focus on the symptom or product of learning. The quandary is that although we might recognise the problem, convincing a data-obsessed profession that we need to promote learning conversation about learning, is very problematic.

The QCDA (2008) suggested that effective curriculum innovation should be disciplined, focused, based on evidence and closely monitored. It has presented a seven-step action learning process, which has been tried and tested in schools (see Figure 4.1 on page 39). This has been developed to help transform the curriculum and ensure changes made have had a positive impact on learners' achievements, lives and prospects. Capturing moments in time can be useful at a variety of points on a learner's journey, by signposting future learning and implications for our teaching. The seven dimensions become tools to help us to learn and progress better: they do not need to be graded as an isolated concept.

Although it has been developed for the secondary curriculum in England, the Disciplined Innovation Process based on an 'action research cycle' is a useful approach to curriculum development in any phase of education in any country.

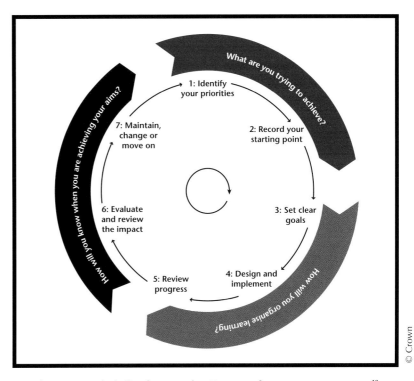

© Crown

Figure 4.1: Disciplined Innovation Process: the seven-step process [10]

Example of base lining and developing positive change within a curriculum using QCDA's seven-step process	
1 Priority	Develop lifelong learners.
2 Starting point	Our review indicated that most of our learner behaviours focus on learning facts and answering questions. Few children demonstrate a reasonable curiosity or creativity, and fewer still ask questions or make suggestions that direct learning. Almost all teacher questions in lessons focus on what needs to be done. Learning to Learn inventory administered.
3 Clear goals	As well as being good at taking tests and passing exams, we also want our learners to: • become independent enquirers and take responsibility for their own learning • be curious and ask questions of us • find creative solutions and be clear about what interests them • develop lines of thinking and show high levels of critical analysis.

4	Design and implement	Curriculum provision was developed to include:
		• 'learning to solve problems' from the physical education programme of study
		• greater opportunity for creativity.
		Professional development support was sourced to develop effective questioning that promoted dialogue rather than just questions and answers.
		Learner independence was promoted by setting regular independent learning tasks in appropriate activities that were progressively more difficult. Skills of independence were the focus for feedback and questioning.
5	Review progress	Progress was monitored in department meetings and reviewed periodically with the assessing pupils' progress (APP) process.
6	Evaluate impact	Impact was evaluated at the end of the academic year using evidence gained from ICT data, captured as part of everyday teaching and learning. The ELLI was also re-administered at the end of the school year.
7	Maintain, change, or move on	The whole process revealed significant progress against targets, but highlighted a lack of teacher understanding and learner awareness of **critical analysis**. A whole-school development day around this area, linked to Masters accreditation in teaching and learning, was planned for the following year.

Figure 4.1 demonstrates how it may be valuable to track learning power to gauge progress towards targets. Any data developed is not intended for comparison with other year groups or other schools in league table format; rather, it is contextual and can help the establishment reflect on the learning culture fostered.

Physical education has wrestled with the concept of quality assessment processes, and good practitioners use curriculum standards appropriately as they were intended. Should any school or subject capture learning power, it need not become a quantitative performance indicator. It is essential that the 'capture of moments in time' is useful to all parties and does not become a frequent data collection exercise where the very essence of its purpose is lost: that of helping learners reflect upon how they are adapting to the variety of learning contexts and situations in which they find themselves.

There are many profiling examples for learning and learning styles, including a range of variable quality questionnaires, which are freely available on the Internet. The following examples have utilised the seven dimensions as a frame of reference. Learners complete a 72-question online profile and an individual spider diagram profile is generated. This can also be represented as a histogram or bar chart. Once produced, it provides a very useful starting point for analysing learning power and for initiating a conversation with learners that helps to effect positive change.

"Reward and celebrate the process pupils have gone through and not just the outcome."

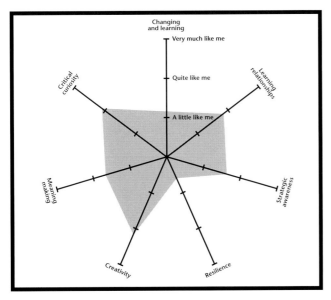

Figure 4.2: Spider diagram profile for a seven-year-old boy

Individual profiling

Accompanying the visual representation of the completed inventory, each individual also receives a narrative and suggested strategies for development.

There are no numbers attached to the spider diagram as in this type of assessment, numbers communicate little;

they are ineffective and often promote feelings of learner inadequacy. The whole purpose is to encourage learners to reflect on how they might change. It is the profile feedback information provided to learners that stimulates a response, and it is the student's response to that feedback that is critical (Deakin Crick, 2006).

An example of using the profile information

From knowing the student in previous physical education settings, a teacher was able to interpret the profile of a seven-year-old boy (Figure 4.2) and use it to reinforce the already strong characteristics of the learner. The teacher was also able to collaborate with the learner in developing the dimensions that were not reflected as strengths. The profile reinforces that the student is highly creative; a curiosity in his work is evident and maybe associated with his creativity. A subsequent discussion related the learner's story to the dimensions and the resulting topography signposted a direction that was helpful to both teacher and learner.

Of particular significance was that the generated learning conversation helped to identify a lack of learner understanding in transferring and applying learning to different contexts and subjects. Of most concern was that the learner seemed to lack resilience. Conversation confirmed that he had a tendency to give up rather easily when presented with problems or difficult tasks. The profile and resulting discussion helped both teacher and learner to develop meaning and to cultivate the concept that learning is learnable. For the pupil it also meant that the door to a range of possible strategies was opened. For example, it was agreed they should work on developing resilience and look at coping strategies to employ when learning got tough. A buddy system was promoted for the pupil to turn to co-learners for support and motivation. As confidence grew, leadership responsibilities were

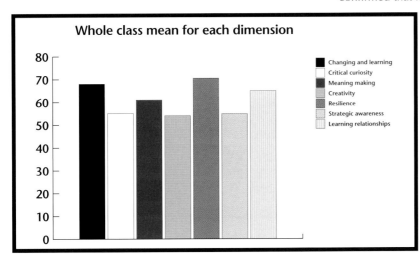

Figure 4.3: Graph showing a Year 7 whole-class position in the seven dimensions

introduced and the pupil was tasked to make decisions about learning in increasingly pressured situations.

Whole-class profiling

It is possible to group individual profiles to give a picture of the whole class (Figure 4.3). However, it is important to remember that the more data grouped together and inferences made, the more the sometimes intricate, personalised learning story is lost. It is necessary, therefore, to analyse groups with a secure knowledge of the group and individuals.

Initial analysis suggests the class appears to be quite resilient and can persevere when learning becomes difficult. Interestingly, the previous individual example from the same class demonstrates there are hidden individual differences. In this case, the individual needs to develop skills in a particular learning dimension, which is generally being displayed as a group strength. The strategic awareness of the class and the creativity both appear quite low and may benefit from future targeted learning. A focus on the seven dimensions and regular reflection on major milestone learning are useful starting points. A range of strategies that actively involve pupils in peer and self-assessment is very worthwhile.

If each of the seven dimensions are examined and class responses analysed it is possible to identify where some pupils may be demonstrating learning power in different ways. For example, Figures 4.4 and 4.5 have probed the whole-class group data. This could be done for any of the seven dimensions but, in this example, resilience and critical curiosity have been presented. A key has been included to allow the reader to easily identify where priority for development may lie. The black bars are the pupils whose profiles suggest they require immediate learning support in the dimension to help them to progress. The pink bars suggest learners would benefit from a targeted and monitored approach, although not necessarily as an immediate priority. The grey bars suggest that pupils are doing well in the dimension and this can be maintained by less frequent checking at various future junctures.

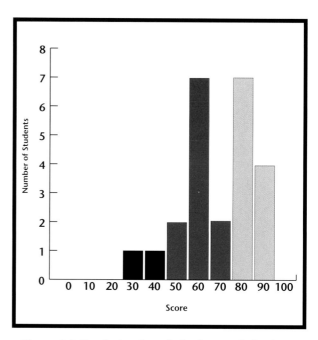

Figure 4.4 Graph showing whole-class analysis of one dimension (resilience)

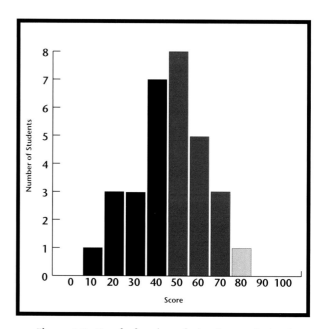

Figure 4.5: Graph showing whole-class analysis of one dimension (critical curiosity)

These pupils could also assist their peers in this dimension. This information should be considered with observations from teaching and learning episodes, and any learner conversation with regard to perceived abilities within that particular dimension.

The class appears to be fairly resilient with only two pupils in the black category. As a class, this dimension can generally be perceived as a strength.

Only two students indicated a critical curiosity in their learning. With the highest number of students appearing in the pink category and 14 pupils in the black area, Figure 4.5 suggests this area of their learning would benefit from a targeted approach. Undertaking this type of analysis for all seven dimensions is a useful exercise in base lining and getting to know learners.

Using the profile information

All of the previous examples are from the same Year 7 physical education class and highlight the way in which the profiles or any other investigative mechanism may be used to construct a learner conversation about developing learning power. This promotes a sense of self-worth and awareness. The learners themselves can take responsibility and have some bearing on their ability to change and grow as a learner.

The data collated from profiling is best considered as the basis for further investigation, rather than taking the results at face value and converting them to a number or a grade. The information is only of use to a particular teacher and a group of learners in a particular context at a moment in time. It is possible to scrutinise differences following intervention using a pre-/post-test method, but all this demonstrates is an association between the intervention strategies and any resulting change over time. Discussion of individual learning gains and further target setting, strengthen a learner's association between strategies tried, success, and growing and changing as a learner. This can only serve to further motivate and inspire.

Implementing change

In order to make a significant difference and cultivate an ethos of change, it is important to embrace the notion of deep learning for all learners in an institution's community of practice (see Chapter 2). Change is likely to be most effective when a whole-school approach is embraced and implemented through subject areas. The narratives in Chapter 5 provide practical examples of this. It is still possible to effect learning power through isolated subject work, but learner impact is greatly reduced.

Learning culture and social conscience

Educational establishments have, for a protracted time, worked in very delicate political environments. They were being held accountable to pupils, parents and the wider community, and judged primarily using a range of attainment data related to rates of progress and academic standards. Primary schools have been publicly judged on SATs and attendance data, while secondary schools have had to report Key Stage 3 SATs results (abolished in 2009) and examination data, with particular importance given to the core subjects. Even contextual value-added data has concentrated on attainment in core subjects. The further education (FE) sector and sixth-form colleges have had to report success rates; for example, the number of students who complete their course against the number starting a course, and the number of students who achieve against the number that are retained. Higher education has been required to ensure students attain good degree classifications. These are all valid indicators of the success of an establishment, but by no means the only criteria against which to judge success. It is vital to start thinking about developing not just the learning but the learner, their life experience and their lifelong learning skills. A social conscience is required that values learners' personal stories and this transcends headline performance data. To that end, it is also important that learners are supported in transition, which will require effective relationship building with other institutions, employers and the learners themselves, and the development of more coherent and effective collaborative practices and processes.

The legacy of this approach is that learners will continue to be effective once they have left establishments; they will be suitably equipped and they will be learners for life.

Reflective Activity

The purpose of this activity is to develop your awareness of yourself and colleagues as learners.

1   Does your establishment have systems in place to monitor the achievements of all learners in this phase?

2   Consider which taxonomy you might use to develop the language of learning with your own learners.

3   How do you or how might you capture 'moments in time' and how does this influence your view of assessment?

4   Analytically discuss with colleagues each of the graphs and diagrams presented in this chapter, and develop your own interpretations.

5   How do you currently collate and review information to plan for personal, learning or thinking skills related to pupil awareness of themselves as learners?

References

Deakin Crick. R. (2006) *Learning Power in Practice: A Guide for Teachers*. London: Paul Chapman Publishing. ISBN: 978-1-412922-20-3.

Frapwell, A. (2006) *Entering New Worlds: From Best Practice to Next Practice*. Worcester: Tacklesport. (CD-ROM)

QCDA (2008) *Disciplined Innovation: Making a Difference to Learners*. ISBN 978-1-84721-733-2.

Sharpe, K. (2008) 'Beyond Classification', *The Times Higher Education*, 24 July 2008.

Further Reading

Websites:

ELLI Learning Profiles and ELEARN: www.ellionline.co.uk

ELLI Research summaries: www.ellionline.co.uk/index.php?id=25

Chapter 5: Learning to Learn Narratives

Purpose

To provide case studies that give insight into the implementation of Learning to Learn principles in action. Each case study is reported in a slightly different way, but the formats are designed to acquaint readers with the important characteristics of each particular circumstance and starting point. As such, the approaches used are contextual; they reflect individual, departmental and institutional thinking and experience, and they represent a moment in time. The case studies are not templates to replicate; rather, they are personalised narratives about a direction followed.

Key Messages

- The catalyst for change doesn't always need to be because something isn't going very well.
- Pupils, teachers and schools all require a sense of direction, active engagement, enquiry and reflection on factors (individual and shared) that influence learning, and the motivation, will and knowledge needed to bring about change.
- Assessment for Learning (AfL) can be a key element and part of the process of Building Learning Power (BLP).
- We can all improve the process of measuring impact – have we made a difference to the learner and has that difference been worthwhile?
- Try things out, embrace a process of disciplined innovation (evidenced-based practice) but don't be afraid to fail and learn from mistakes.
- Teachers and schools need to develop the processes and practices of Learning to Learn in their own learning if they are to create the conditions to build learning power for all pupils (parallel processes).

Christian Malford C of E Primary School, Chippenham, Wiltshire

Background

Christian Malford C of E Primary School is a small rural school in North Wiltshire on the banks of the River Avon near Chippenham. It has 80 pupils organised into three classes and an even number of boys and girls. Pupils come from a wide range of social, economic and academic backgrounds. Only 27% of pupils are eligible for free school meals, which is below the national average and reflects the advantaged background of many of the pupils. Few children speak English as an additional language. When children start school, their skills, knowledge and understanding are very wide ranging; most children have reached the levels expected for their age, with some doing much better and some a little behind.

Commensurate with the national average, 19% of pupils have been identified as having special educational needs.

School ethos

The school prides itself on being a happy school where children can enjoy learning and everyone is respected. Ofsted (November, 2004) reported 'pupils are very happy at Christian Malford C of E Primary School. They really enjoy learning and behave very well'.

The school promotes a culture of fun and enjoyment while promoting high standards. Central to this is the philosophy that learning is the key to everything carried out. Everyone in the school is engaged in the belief that they are on a 'learning treasure hunt'. This voyage of discovery encourages the use of the skills needed to help learning in three ways:

- **Learning skills for independence**: the school helps individuals become more aware of themselves as learners and promotes active engagement in learning; for example, listening and what to do when learning gets stuck.

- **Learning skills for interdependence**: skills needed to work with others, such as discussion, planning and presenting are promoted. Thinking skills are very useful so the school explores such activities as creative ideas and mind mapping.

- **Reflection:** staff and pupils reflect on their **voyage of learning** and decide individually and collaboratively what they need to do next to make themselves even better learners.

In September 2006, this approach to learning was central to the school winning the Young Archaeologist of the Year Award for the children's work on the history of the school. The curriculum is devised into cross-subject topics, which helps learners link and make sense of the content, while assisting in promoting skills; for example, numeracy and literacy, in different ways.

The starting point

In 2004, an audit of children's learning skills indicated poor independence and a lack of perseverance on tasks. The school's Ofsted inspection that year confirmed some of the areas raised by the audit.

> 'We were good at delivering or presenting information to learners, we were good at covering content, but we weren't effective in developing learners as learners – we did not develop their learning skills.'
>
> Head teacher
> Christian Malford C of E Primary School

The Christian Malford C of E Primary School staff got together and decided their aim was to ensure that learning skills would be integrated into the curriculum. They wanted their learners to engage more and take greater ownership of learning.

What the school did

Professional development

Information assimilated and evaluated from the school review of professional practice (required for the School Evaluation Form) and the Ofsted report, combined to signpost a clear way forward for learning. The school coordinated professional development for staff, based around Guy Claxton's four Rs (Reflectiveness, Reciprocity, Resilience and Resourcefulness)[11]. Being a small school, this was achieved by creating a rural cluster consisting of seven schools. Staff from the various schools each tried out their own ideas, giving them ownership of the process. Interestingly, staff viewed themselves as learners in this process and utilised this knowledge to apply to their own contexts. A situation of parallel processes had developed. Teachers were learners first and this insight into learning processes gave them a greater understanding of their own attributes as well as those of the pupils.

Treasure hunt

At Christian Malford C of E Primary School, staff developed problem-based work, centred on topics. For example, in history the topic might be the Tudors, but the skill process is investigation. In physical education, the topic might be space finding in relation to themselves, others and equipment, but the skill process might be reflectiveness. Central to this development was the conviction that learning could be related to a treasure hunt: learning could and should be fun and exciting; it could be made to feel like a **journey of discovery**. This treasure hunt analogy led to the creation of roles, which helped learners identify and grow aware of their particular strengths and areas to address as learners. Children developed this idea and created their own associations; for example, a cat was allied with curiosity.

Learning Olympics

The learning analogy led to the school developing further ideas, including a Learning Olympics where learners' skills in the four Rs were developed. This approach led to learners and teachers devising a simple set of graded statements within each of the four R categories. Children had the opportunity to achieve as bronze, silver and gold learners.

[11] See Chapter 3.

> 'We weren't afraid to think outside the box, we were constantly looking to broker exciting ideas for learning. We devised engaging topics and focused on the processes to achieve better outcomes. Communication with learners went beyond content and coverage – we saw children very much as partners in the learning process.'
>
> Head teacher
> Christian Malford C of E Primary School

The Learning Monster game

A further co-constructed development has been the Learning Monster game. Children are encouraged to recognise 'monsters' that prevent them from engaging with their learning. They use their imagination to draw these monsters and what they might look like and at times they physically 'zap' the monsters to kinaesthetically eradicate their threat. Other strategies include anticipating and discussing how they might deal with, for example, the distracting monster.

Parallel processes

> 'Teachers were allowed to discuss teaching and matters...their dialogue was allowed to go "off the radar".'

This type of approach also manifested itself in the writing of the School Development plan (SDP), centred on Every Child Matters (ECM): it is written with the children. One pupil volunteers from each year group and helps to set priorities and targets. Children interview the head teacher to monitor progress against the development plan objectives. Reflection occurs at multiple levels: children are involved in a lot of peer and self-assessment. This advance was also evident in a change to homework policy. Many children, indeed some parents, thought the homework was pointless. What developed was home learning. Children were given home-learning folders and tasks that were devised with the teachers. One type of task involved children and parents watching certain

programmes, having a discussion about them and devising questions about the programmes, using the discussion as a stimulus to reinforce, extend and even introduce topic work in school.

Measuring whole-school impact

Outcome

The school is building evidence over time and it is important to distinguish certain terms. With regard to a difference in outcomes, there is an improvement in pupil attitudes, attributes, behaviours and learning. All teachers are commenting on this. Everything is more focused and appears joined up. Children and teachers are more engaged, there is noticeably less behavioural problems and, socially and emotionally, children are able to cope with the demands of learning: they know what to do when they get stuck, they are more determined and persevere at a task, they can help each other and are not afraid to ask for help. Of particular note is that they are more confident – they actually engage in tasks knowing they will get better at something. These are attributable, to a large extent, to the improvement in teacher outputs as a result of their professional development input and continuing professional or learning dialogue. Children are heavily involved in peer and self-assessment. They can plan for and recognise progress; they are partners in the process. The bronze, silver and gold progressive statements aren't used to teach to; rather, they are statements that are referred to in order to monitor milestone progress. Learners took ownership of developing the statements, they are fully engaged in the process of learning and fully involved in monitoring progress and a sample of children are interviewed as part of an ongoing review.

Impact

Whereas an outcome is a change in pupil learning resulting from teacher outputs, impact refers to broader, longer-term change and relates to the SDP. In terms of SDP targets, the impact at Christian Malford C of E Primary School cannot be measured in the relatively short time the school has embarked on the process of Learning to Learn.

A Learning to Learn approach is one of a number of contributory outcomes that will help to assess long-term change or impact.

What we did in physical education

'Developing our awareness as and of learners really helped our teaching of physical education. Previously, we were perhaps too focused on sports outcomes and our developing knowledge of processes resulted in a renewed approach and a greater confidence towards promoting learning in the subject.'

Primary Link Tutor

Audit and action

Physical education was the last subject to come onboard with regards to Learning to Learn. With the benefit of hindsight we could perhaps have started earlier. We carried out a survey or an audit on BLP. We wanted children to reflect in more depth on their learning and progress, and signpost ways forward. The audit was a start to this process. Children were fully involved. This didn't mean we had to take time out of physical education. This could be done in other lessons; for example, literacy or during circle time in personal and social health. Through signposting, we helped children by pre-fixing our learning outcomes with the phrase 'I know I will have been successful if...' This really helped us as teachers and the children as learners. Children were more occupied and on task; they were confident to comment about things, confident to get involved and ask questions. We are not saying this never happened previously; rather, it was more focused, more engaging, and more inclusive. When we started this approach in physical education, staff were neither reluctant nor reticent, they were more worried how they could develop Learning to Learn in a physical

education context. Staff were going to be out of their comfort zone. What we did was to develop the positive assumption that we were already doing it in physical education. We wanted staff to unpack what they were doing, raise their awareness of themselves as learners and the way they were teaching the subject. It was possible for everyone to say 'yes' because, in some form or another, there are Learning to Learn processes integrated into the way we frame learning in physical education. This provided the springboard for professional dialogue about practice and how we developed it. The whole process has been one great professional development exercise, without the need to constantly go out on courses.

One thing we did notice was a difference in children's attitudes and engagement in literacy – they were speaking and listening with interest, with a purpose and they were enthusiastic. The evaluating and improving aspect in physical education really did lend itself to promoting literacy through physical education in this way. This has also had an influence in terms of writing skills as our standards have risen to well above the national average. This approach is a continuous improvement process and improving children's listening, articulation of learning and peer- and self-assessment provide a constant focus.

Key features

Key features of practice that were developed included leadership through physical education, ICT in physical education, topic-based learning and coaching and mentoring processes. In terms of the four Rs, Table 4 is an insight into what we saw in terms of outcomes for children.

The focus on learners as learners helped staff to approach physical education in a more confident

Table 4: Summary of the four Rs in practice			
Resilience	**Reflection**	**Resourcefulness**	**Relationships**
'This was perhaps the easiest R to notice. Children would stick at learning even though it was difficult. We would encourage them, but they would also encourage each other. The outdoor residential programme we run really helps develop this component because some of the problems are designed so that there is no right or wrong answer or that it is impossible to complete. We learn so much about children through this work, and if the plenary is skilfully conducted, they learn a lot about themselves.'	'We linked this very much to the evaluating and improving aspect and knowledge and understanding of fitness and health from the physical education processes. We ensure children are aware of the level they are working commensurate with. It is not about the level, rather, that they know how to improve their performance in order to progress through the level and they constantly get better at doing this. Those learners who see this as an ongoing skill can apply and adapt their learning to different contexts. They become better at Learning to Learn for themselves.'	'In physical education we found learners who are resourceful will be innovative; they will be creative and are the children who come up with the ideas, draw on other experiences and use them to be successful at whatever task they are working on. The challenge we faced was to ensure all learners had opportunity to develop this area and not be dominated by those with all the ideas. "Solutions" included small group working to allow a collaborative response and learners taking on leadership roles linked to making decisions.'	'Part of our school ethos is to develop learner independence and interdependence. The ability to work alone and with others is important in physical education with regards to the range of activity areas, but also in other lessons and for life beyond school! Physical education is an area where it is easy to provide opportunity to develop these skills and children really do engage – especially in the course of the one week outdoor residential programme. Whether it is rocket building or kayaking, we see learners who are willing to share ideas with others or stand back and observe.'
'Much of this stuff (the four Rs) is interrelated – we have developed this through activity and talk. We monitor this to ensure an even-handed approach and a rounded learner.'			

manner. There was something to grasp – all children were learners, we were all learners, the four aspects in physical education are processes and we can develop these processes so children can get better at learning activities for themselves.

Something to celebrate

Although it was not our overriding target, one of the biggest areas for us to celebrate was winning the local football and rugby cups. We are a small school and draw on a small population, so the achievement was even more discernable, especially as we hadn't won anything for a while – certainly not a football cup. Our learners aren't the best footballers, but they believe in themselves as learners, they understand themselves as learners and this promoted attitudes to learning and competition that have made them winners.

"When undertaking a small piece of work show how this relates to the bigger picture."

A developing culture

With the advent of the Learning Outside the Classroom (LOtC) manifesto, physical education has taken on a greater profile in the school. Our outdoor residential programme promotes the Learning to Learn process. Children are learning in and through physical education. Staff learn to learn better from each other. One example is the Year 3 and 4 Outward Bound work we do. All children, in particular those with dyslexia and learning difficulties, have really benefited. We see this in their raised self-esteem, improved confidence and, above all, their resilience or their ability to really stick at learning when it gets difficult. Another example of the influence this approach has had is that we are now a leading Healthy School, currently working on a project to promote and develop long-distance walking.

Although we have only recently been focusing on this area, there is a learning culture growing throughout everything we do. The school philosophy promotes an ethos, but it is the staff and pupils who have taken ownership of it. Connections are strong and the culture is embedding and beginning to enhance everything we do.

Outwood Grange Academy, Wakefield, West Yorkshire

Background

Outwood Grange Academy (OGA) is one of the largest secondary schools/colleges in the country. Students come from the northern area of Wakefield and nearby villages where there is an average mix of social and economic conditions. Some 95% of students are of White British background. Several Asian minority ethnic groups largely account for the remaining 5%. Students' attainment on entry to the school is slightly higher than the national average. The proportion of students with learning difficulties and/or disabilities, or with statements of special educational need is below average. The school achieved

Technology College status in 2002, Training School in 2003 and Applied Learning Specialism status in 2008.

In its 2006 inspection report, Grade 1 (outstanding) was achieved in all categories (Overall Effectiveness of School, Achievement and Standards, Quality of Provision, Leadership and Management). The full report can be found on the OGA website.

Background to the introduction of Learning to Learn

OGA has been developing ideas, programmes of study and experiences linked to Learning to Learn or deep learning for approximately 10 years.

A greater focus for understanding learning was developed with the pilot scheme for the University of the First Age (UFA) in 2001. A number of schools were asked to embrace the idea of exploring what learning meant, key parts to learning, how it could be accelerated and how they could move to become lifelong learners. Two members of staff from OGA were asked to take part in this new initiative. Their role in the initial instance was to gain an understanding of the concepts delivered by the UFA and then translate them into practical teaching advice and guidance for staff. The additional aspect of the course was funding for three summer schools.

The summer school's focus group was made up of students who were underachieving, or those struggling with school and needing new vigour to appreciate that they could learn how to learn better. The cohort was made up of students from Years 6 and 7. The programme was a week long with a spotlight on the **multiple intelligences** and a healthy lifestyle to improve behaviour, memory and performance. The theme of the last two summer schools was the Olympic Games: students were given a country to investigate, for which they had to create a presentation, and develop and work on a new sport for that country. Their job was then to present this to the other groups and teach them their new sport.

In terms of teaching and learning, the concepts from the UFA have gone further than initially expected as now there is real focus on Learning to Learn and behaviour for learning. Learning and the different aspects of it have become part of the nine gateways in education, and this linked with other areas such as Gifted and Talented and Student Voice make up deep learning. At OGA, deep learning has been embraced so much that there is a separate leadership structure, which focuses on moving and shaping the curriculum and young people so that they can be lifelong learners who are able and equipped to learn in whatever context.

The OGA approach to developing deep learning: A snapshot of activity by timeline

- 2001: UFA training was undertaken.

- Summer schools were implemented from 2002–2004.

- Delivery to staff at whole college meetings, initially on the different learning styles and how to incorporate them occurred from 2004 onwards.

- Departments reviewed practice and focused on different types of learners and more creative lessons.

- An AfL policy was developed.

- Delivery to students in Year 11 were taught about how to learn and how to revise – supporting exam planning and preparation was developed as a one-hour carousel of delivery.

- A working party was established on lessons for learning which developed a structure that all staff could follow that would enhance the learning experience and explore the accelerated learning cycle (Smith, 2000). This was rolled out in 2005 when all departments followed the set plan and all lesson plans were written to embrace this cycle.

- An observation proforma promoted a variety of learning and is part of the five-part lesson – if it is not used in lessons then it is deemed unsatisfactory.

- Members of the working party delivered to Initial Teacher Trainees (ITT), Newly Qualified Teachers and Graduate Training Programme students. This is ongoing.

- Members of OGA were invited to Leeds University to speak to ITT students about learning styles and the impact it can have in the classroom. This started in 2005 and is ongoing.

- A working party was set up to try and develop Learning to Learn in an out of school context (2005). Students engage in project work for two hours a week. These students are selected from the 'Praising Stars' system – those who are underachieving or lacking in effort and motivation.

- A Year 7 half day on learning styles and how they can learn better was introduced in 2006.

- OGA was awarded the Yorkshire and Humberside Learning Hub – this allowed coordination with other schools to develop a policy and procedure for learning.

- Deep learning has been established in the college as well as other 'deeps' (2007).

- A Deep Learning Plan of Action for improving learning in and out of college has been developed.

- A Learning Model (Figure 5.1 on page 52) was created with five skills and five qualities that the college identified its students needed to develop in order to be lifelong learners. Learning outcomes should focus on this Learning Model.

- Students in Year 7 have 'deep learning lessons' once a week in relation to the Learning Model then practise and develop their skills and qualities in relation to project type learning.

So how did this relate to physical education?

Sport education was introduced to years 7 and 8 following work conducted by the advanced skills teacher in the primary schools through the school sports coordinator programme. Work on leadership, whether it be Wake up and Shake up, Fitbods or similar activities, extend into the curriculum.

Respectful

Resilient

Investigate

Listen

Co-operate **Independent**

Communicate

Creative **Confident**

Organise

ESTABLISHING A CULTURE OF DEEP LEARNING

Figure 5.1: The OGA Learning Model

Downend School, Downend, South Gloucestershire

Background

Downend School is a large, mixed 11–18 comprehensive school in Bristol, South Gloucestershire. It has had Technology Specialist College status since 1999. The school is committed to achieving the highest academic standards, leading developments in education and technology, and in preparing students for their academic and vocational career pathways. To achieve this, the school works in partnership with a consortium of local schools to provide post-14 courses. Students are drawn from 27 primary and junior schools. There are 1800 pupils including the sixth form and this relates to 270 Year 7 pupils split into nine tutor groups. The proportion of pupils with learning difficulties or disabilities is slightly above the national average; each year, on average, 30 students have statements of special educational needs. The majority of pupils enter the school with broadly average attainment.

Core values

Downend School aims to provide each student with their own personal pathway to success. The core values that underpin this are focused on a sense of belonging, a belief that all students have it within themselves to be effective learners and that this learning can be extended beyond the reach of school and into the future. In striving to achieve this, the school has developed a Learning to Learn approach, which fosters the collaborative skills learners bring from their primary years and further develops their ability to learn in a variety of ways. The school aims to give students the skills needed for problem solving, thinking, and working independently and in teams. Perhaps more importantly, it gives learners a voice.

Students follow a Young Leaders Awards scheme, which lays the Foundation to the BTEC Certificate in years 9 and 10 and which all students follow. To achieve an award, a large section of the scheme is devoted to coaching and leading both peers and primary students. The Sports Leaders UK level one award is followed in Year 11 and the level two award and Higher Sports Leadership are options in the sixth form. The sport education programme has been well received by all abilities. This concept has been extended into the accredited BTEC programme. The planning and leading section of the course has developed students into independent learners and thinkers, as they have to take into account the various learning styles of their peers.

**Interview with Lawrence Dorman –
a teacher's perspective**

Q: The school seeks to promote and support all learners. Can you give me an insight into the key features of this approach?

A: One of the things driving what we do is personalising the student learning experience. With reference to Hargreaves' (2005) four deeps, **deep learning** is about student voice, AfL and Learning to Learn. We are constantly looking to improve provision for learners to develop in all of these areas and these need to be addressed as an integrated whole for deep learning to be developed.

Q: Can you tell me more about the approach to student voice?

A: The school promotes learner voice and this can be student or teacher voice. At Downend School we are all learners. We promote opportunity for students to share who they are, what they believe and why they believe what they do, with their peers, parents, teachers and the entire school. The student voice is engaged in numerous ways, in classrooms and beyond the school, and this is something that is evolving as we develop ideas in practice and learn from the process. A large part of student voice is about action. So at Downend School we have students who have been part of focus groups about their learning and about AfL. This means that students will take on tasks according to their role, to help deliver a better education to their present and future peers. The student voice is developing quite successfully, as the school culture and ethos have really shifted to cultivate and support the learners and their needs, and the integration and expansion of activities in response to learner needs and curriculum changes.

Encouraging student participation is as beneficial to staff as it is to students. Students may not always describe school as their favourite place, but the more student voice we have in school, the more enjoyable it becomes. Through the gradual building of confidence and skills, the students are able to work more effectively in partnership with staff to improve the school for everyone's benefit.

As a school we have been working to:

- empower students to use technology with confidence
- widen the awareness of the student voice
- develop student representatives' roles within the school
- gather students' opinions on school improvement
- establish a link between the senior leadership team and student voice
- establish online communication as a method of choice for students.

In physical education these areas have provided a useful focus and have manifested themselves in practice as learners have a choice about which activities they follow, and a choice about their learning direction in lessons. We are in discussion as a department about physical education councils so that there is a student input into decisions about curriculum design, choice and coherence.

Q: So where does AfL fit into all of this?

A: As mentioned previously, learner voice has been promoted through a variety of different activities, not least during lessons and this has linked to our promotion of AfL strategies and the use of four main actions of questioning to promote dialogue, feedback, success criteria, and peer and self-assessment. Combinations of these actions promote greater learner engagement in lessons and this, linked with opportunities for reflection, is exactly what we wanted to do. Above all, we wanted our learners in physical education to be more responsible for their own and others' learning, to become more independent as opposed to constantly asking us how to do things and to support each other and work cooperatively. We began to talk about assessment as being the language of learning or perhaps more appropriately a **language for learning**. We, (staff and learners) are continuously increasing our vocabulary, constantly improving our methods of communication in regards to the actions above and engaging learners more. I think we have really improved as learners first and then in our approaches to the teaching of physical education. Our teaching style has moved on. Teachers are more confident, in that we are not afraid to try things out: we are not afraid to fail. This has all helped us get to know our strengths better; we have got to know learners better and we are beginning to understand the processes and involve learners in these more through peer- and self-assessment.

This has helped our thinking about how and in what form we present information to learners – like visual (writing and images), auditory and kinaesthetic. We provide much more opportunity in lessons for learners to take on a variety of roles, such as leaders, coaches, timekeepers, umpires etc, and in terms of learner involvement, we try to develop awareness of a starting point for learning in a lesson or unit of work. Children are involved in target setting from that starting point and then take greater ownership of decisions made along the way. The problem-solving approach we utilised in Outdoor and Adventurous Activities (now Learning to Problem Solve) helped promote this process and as teachers we found it easier to promote and involve learners in the process. This realisation, I think, has helped the way we look at the teaching of games or outwitting for example. It moves us away from sports outcomes or end-gaming and focuses us much more on the process skills. The advent of the secondary curriculum (2007) and the new 'range and content' has helped us to promote greater opportunity, greater engagement and greater active and situated learning than we have achieved previously. This has emerged in our sport education offer for years 7 and 8. Our philosophy here isn't about the sport or the games played, rather the processes of physical education learners are engaged with; in particular, decision making and differing roles. It might appear a little anecdotal, but this approach, linked with the fact that we gave some

opportunity for our Year 8s to choose their invasion game, has resulted in all pupils bringing kit, all pupils being more fully involved, and this is a marked improvement and a great starting point.

Q: How did this lead to Learning to Learn?

A: We work collaboratively with a number of different schools in our 14–19 curriculum provision. This arrangement also helps us share ideas with other schools and benchmark our progress against them. Professional conversation raised awareness of Learning to Learn gaining kudos in education, leading to rising standards. It mapped to our philosophy, focusing on the learner and our school aims. One of our senior management team had experience of Learning to Learn, and this internal expertise was utilised to assist in the implementation of a Learning to Learn approach at Downend School. Our Learning to Learn programme underpins the curriculum at Key Stage 3 (years 7–9).

Q: Can you describe the implementation process?

A: We used in-house expertise and held a staff training day that introduced the concept of Learning to Learn. This centred on Gardner's theory of multiple intelligences: SELF smart, PICTURE Smart, MUSIC Smart, WORD Smart, LOGIC Smart, NATURE Smart, BODY Smart and PEOPLE Smart. We then presented information to parents at a parents evening and involved them in our thinking behind the change in our whole-school approach to learning. The Student Voice was consulted as we have discussed earlier. The result of this consultation was that the school community (parents, teachers and pupils) wanted to ensure integration with the personal development curriculum (PDC). This was viewed as crucial in underpinning effective learning, positive behaviour and attendance, staff effectiveness, emotional health and well-being, and positive relationships. We divided our Year 7 programme into four themes:

- A place to learn (setting the context for learning)
- Learning to be together (social skills and empathy)
- Keep on learning (motivation)
- Learning about me (understanding and managing feelings).

As a head of year, this made complete sense to me, because my inbox is always full of behaviour problems to deal with. There was a sense of treating the symptom rather than addressing the cause and seeking a cure. I know it might sound trite, but this approach really helped us, well, certainly me, to frame an approach to learners as learners and learners as real people as opposed to paper referrals and issues to deal with. In physical education the house system and the reward system really does help promote positive behaviours and this has now been enhanced, with learners feeling their opinions were valued as a result of a questionnaire we distributed to Year 7. This has helped us to broadly map knowledge requirements, learning needs and wants of Year 7 learners.

Last year, we implemented this blended approach for Year 7 and we followed up with staff training. Currently, years 7 and 8 will follow the Learning to Learn opportunities provided. In Year 8 this is developed slightly with focused **immersion days** with the attention on learners and the learning process.

> Q: What did you learn from the first year
>   of implementation?

A: We carried out a review of the first year of our Learning to Learn approach, and one of the alarming things that became apparent to us was that we didn't have AfL sufficiently embedded in practice. This initially came as a surprise to us, but on reflection, our practice was not consistent enough.

Children, although involved in peer- and self-assessment, were not involved beyond what we might term a superficial level and their confidence to engage and explore processes didn't provide them with a strong enough platform to engage further in a meta-learning context. What we are aspiring to, therefore, is greater knowledge and understanding (a working knowledge) of the processes involved and greater knowledge of our learners so greater consistency can be ensured. What we have noticed so far, however, can be summarised in three key points:

1 **Behaviour is better:** Learners are more engaged, they are more involved and they are taking on more roles and responsibilities. They are more involved in the AfL process and understanding what they are trying to achieve.

2 **Learner-centred approach:** Our practice really is learner centred. The onus is on the learner by increasing their curiosity, getting them to ask questions and promoting the opportunity to succeed.

3 **Progress:** I go back to the promoting a sense of ownership and opportunity example through activity choice and a sport education approach. When you have learners who want to be present, who understand themselves as learners, understand the processes and the key skills involved, and understand the relevance and purpose of these, not just in subjects, but in life, then it is pretty obvious there are less distractions and greater progress. When they are also responsible for decision making; for example, when they have to recognise where they are, discuss their targets, forge learning pathways to meet these targets and know how they are progressing and deal with learning problems on the way, then we are doing our job and it makes the job much easier. We are facilitating their learning and their skills as learners. I am not saying we have this cracked; we have a long way to go, but we have also come a long way in a short time.

> Q: What did you do as a result of your review?

A: We have now appointed an advanced skills teacher who is developing AfL practices. These need to be embedded and enhanced as they are essential in developing meta-learning or Learning to Learn. Our curriculum design is developing to support deep learning and our teaching and learning is utilising ICT so it is used consistently and strategically. Mentoring and coaching for staff are also being investigated just as we promote peer- and self-assessment for learners.

What enthuses me about the physical education staff is that there is an inherent aspiration to develop knowledge about learning practices, so that a consistency can be advanced. Our practice is still a bit ad hoc, but we understand why we are doing what we are doing.

University of Central Lancashire, Preston, Lancashire

A changing approach to learning within higher education

The BA (Hons) Sports Coaching programme at the University of Central Lancashire has been running for approximately 12 years. During this time, the course curriculum and content has been modified to reflect the marketplace and the currency of the award. During this relatively short period, the course team has considered many pedagogical methodologies to enhance the quality of the student experience and, more importantly, to maximise the learning process. This approach is not motivated through the need for change. It represents a mindset open to new ideas. There have been no concerns regarding the course or individual modules on this programme. In fact, students are always very complimentary about the course. So why look for change?

It has been recognised that the traditional lecture/seminar approach contributes to the stifling of learning, through a particularly behaviourist approach to instruction and information overload. Therefore, the team is always on the lookout for ways to improve this. Exposure to the Learning to Learn paradigms afforded the opportunity to revise the pedagogical approach to teaching and create a better emotional and motivational experience. In order to test the intuitively appealing Learning to Learn dimensions, it was

decided to focus on one module, and modify the content delivery in relation to these dimensions. The chosen module was TL3043: High Performance Coaching. As the students have been complimentary about this module in the past, it was decided to retain the module content. Also, the lecture/seminar approach was changed into a two-hour workshop. Although this reduced the financial viability of the module, it increased the flexibility to be adventurous and exploratory in pursuing the Learning to Learn dimensions.

In order to illustrate the changes that have been made, certain sessions will be used to demonstrate the previous delivery and the new approach.

Session one: high performance environments – the way we do things around here

Workshop outcomes:

- To appreciate the importance of coaching philosophy and its influence on behaviour.
- To have a protocol for creating appropriate organisational environments.

Previous approach:

The module tutor would deliver a lecture on coaching philosophy, values and beliefs and their translation into coaching practice. As part of this lecture, motivational climate and leadership behaviour would be included. During the seminar, the students would discuss Mageau & Vallerand (2003) on the coach–athlete relationship. Students would then be required to reflect on this and put forward suggestions with regard to implications for practice.

Evaluation:
Limited student involvement and linkage to the students' reality.

Utilising a Learning to Learn approach:

Students listened to a 10-minute presentation on coaching philosophy using top coaches to illustrate what they believe in, and how this transcends coaching practice. Students were placed into functional groups (based on their interests), and asked to identify an organisation they would take charge of. Typical scenarios were: football academies and first teams or multi-sport coaching companies for kids. We even had a new National Olympic Committee called Fûnnlánd! In these groups, students were asked to articulate their personal values and beliefs. The group was then tasked to devise an organisational mission statement/philosophy. The course tutor provided examples so students could refine their mission statement. Once this was developed students had to identify the main drivers to take their organisation forward, and then begin to identify specific tasks that would see the realisation of their mission statement. These drivers and tasks were written onto Post-It notes and placed on a flipchart.

Each group/organisation then fed back to the workshop group. Rather than present a mission statement, the national Olympic Committee of Fûnnlánd drew a flag and created a national anthem, which was ridiculed by the rest of the class. However, they had great fun and

realised that flags and national anthems are, in fact, metaphors of the organisational philosophy of a nation.

The tutor finished the session by asking the students to now consider their coaching philosophy and the way they coach. 'Did the behaviours that you engaged in match your philosophy?' The tutor asked how this translated into their own coaching practice. It was great to see the students had made the leap between the organisational philosophy and specific tasks, to coaching philosophy and coaching practice. Furthermore, the students thoroughly enjoyed the tasks and engaged throughout the whole two hours.

Evaluation:

This was a great way to influence **learning relationships** by encouraging groups to work together to formulate a shared set of values. The task was excellent at encouraging **critical curiosity** in that the process forced you to delve deeper into philosophy and specifics of organisational operations. The task certainly encouraged **creativity**, because the students were developing organisations and tasks. Some of the ideas were very creative (the flag and national anthem). The other major dimension that was developed was **meaning making**. Being able to translate the organisational philosophy and specific tasks into students' personal coaching philosophy and practice was the major aim of the session. Students certainly left the session questioning their philosophy and how they currently coach. In some cases, this has led to changes in the coaching behaviour of some students. This is incredibly positive, and all from this one session.

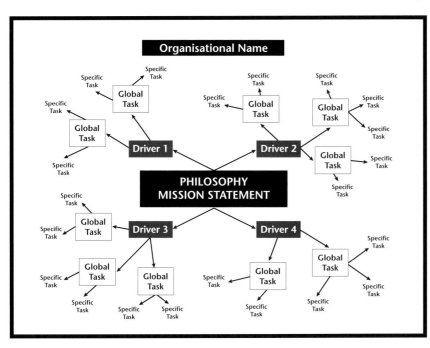

Figure 5.2: Philosophy Mission Statement

Session two: competition preparation – no stone left unturned!

Workshop Outcome:

To critically appreciate the detail and multidisciplinary requirements of effective competition preparation.

Previous approach:

The course tutor would provide a lecture on competition planning followed by students choosing a competition and developing a multidisciplinary plan for a sport of his or her choice. The plan was then presented to the group, and issues were raised by staff and students.

Evaluation:
This was considered to be a very interactive and fun session for the students. It certainly does meet some of the Learning to Learn dimensions; however, the main issue was a simple one. By this stage, the students did not know how to periodise a plan, and didn't really have a grasp of the detail required in a pro-active planning process for competition.

Utilising a Learning to Learn approach:

Students were asked to bring all of the equipment and food items to create the ultimate cheese sandwich. The brief was:

- You will be required to supply a cheese sandwich to the University of Central Lancashire High Performance Coaching Cheese Sandwich Fête.

- The sandwich must be as fresh as possible and you must present it in as appealing a fashion as possible.

- You will be judged on:

    – the appearance of the sandwich

    – the combination of ingredients

    – your selling pitch about the sandwich ('This is not just a cheese sandwich…')

    – your perceived evaluation of taste.

Students arrived with all of the ingredients and implements to create the sandwich. Some students dressed up for the

event, as did the course tutor. He wore a white coat and a bakery hat with a clipboard. Students were given 15 minutes to create, garnish and present the sandwich. Half the group were then asked to stand by their sandwich while the other half peer reviewed the sandwiches along with the course tutor. The winner was awarded a jar of Branston pickle and a jar of Hellmann's mayonnaise.

The activity was a success and the students had a really good time. On a more serious educational note, some of the students turned up with a pre-packaged sandwich. Others brought all the ingredients but forgot the implements to create the sandwich. The activity was debriefed by staff and students. Students were asked to identify the parallels between this activity and competition preparation.

Evaluation:
Both the previous task and the Learning to Learn task were enjoyed by the students. It was felt that the Learning to Learn activity was pitched at an appropriate level and progressed the learner's knowledge on competition preparation. The activity utilised a great deal of creativity to develop the best sandwich, but was also a great vehicle for enhancing competition preparation knowledge. This activity drew directly from the meaning making dimension. Here we used the metaphor of the perfect sandwich to explore the perfect competition preparation. Finally, the task was individual in nature, but the speed dating approach to the peer review allowed students to examine his or her efforts in relation to the efforts of others, thus developing the learning relationships aspect of the Learning to Learn dimensions.

Summary

The examples described above represent just two modifications to a 24-week scheme of work. Although the indicative content has not changed, the teaching team feel strongly that they have created activities that are enjoyable, engaging and educationally progressive in fulfilling the learning outcomes of the module. The students have thoroughly enjoyed both workshops.

"Let talking about how you feel in physical education become the norm!"

Although there is no formal assessment of the module by the students, anecdotal evidence and the energy clearly evident in sessions would suggest that enhancing the workshops with a focus on, not only the learning content, but the learner experience and their learning skills (with reference to the seven dimensions) will be encouraged across the whole curriculum in the future.

Reflective Activity

The purpose of this activity is to consider the rationale, key challenges and the importance of readiness factors in adopting a Learning to Learn approach.

1   Describe the key features that are common across each case study.

2   What would be your rationale for implementing a Learning to Learn approach?

3   List elements of your work that already reflect a Learning to Learn approach.

4   Identify key readiness factors for implementation that your school already has.

5   What would be the key challenges you expect to face?

6   What changes to your teaching and learning would you expect to make?

7   How would you expect to collect evidence of outcomes or impact?

References

Hargreaves, D. (2005) *Personalising Learning 3: Learning to Learn and the New Technologies*. London: Specialist Schools Trust. ISBN: 978-1-905150-18-0.

Gardner, G. (1993) *Frames of Mind. The theory of multiple intelligences*, Basic Books: New York. ISBN: 978-0-465025-10-7.

Mageau, G.A. and Vallerand, R.J. (2003) 'The coach–athlete relationship: a motivational model'. *Journal of Sports Sciences*, 21: 883–904.

Further Reading

Websites:

Christian Malford C of E Primary School: www.christianmalford.wilts.sch.uk

Outwood Grange Academy: http://grange.outwood.com

Downend Secondary School: www.downend.com

University of Central Lancashire: www.uclan.ac.uk

Secondary National Strategy: www.nationalstrategies.org.uk/Home.aspx

Chapter 6: Learning to Learn: Practical Examples

Purpose

The purpose of this chapter is to provide several practical examples of how the Learning to Learn concept (specifically the Effective Lifelong Learning Inventory [ELLI] dimensions) has been used in physical education learning episodes. Each practical example presents the challenge that was identified and a strategy involving a number of actions that was put into place. The dimension(s) targeted or utilised are highlighted. What you, the reader, are encouraged to do is to use these examples to develop your thinking and ideas about practice.

Key Messages

- A set of isolated practices does not constitute a Learning to Learn approach. The examples given here are to highlight where Learning to Learn ideas might already be present in your practice and to promote further ideas. They should form part of a strategic whole-school approach.

- Although the examples refer to particular situations, the concepts and ideas, with careful reflection, can be adopted and adapted to different contexts.

- Creating a learner-centred physical education environment and rounded learners requires an understanding of the processes, knowledge of the learner and a range of coordinated practical strategies.

- Interventionist approaches do not always have to be implemented because there is a real or perceived weakness to address. The decision to intervene might be because there are ways of doing things that will really challenge and engage all learners in the learning processes and develop existing good practice.

Practical Examples – Primary Schools

Strategic Awareness and Meaning Making

The challenge

A teacher was appointed to a primary link teacher (PLT) post. A physical education and school sport programme, which had been in place for 12 years, existed at the school. The curriculum provision; ie how it was taught and assessed, had remained virtually the same, despite statutory changes to the curriculum in 1995 and 1999. The focus of teaching activities over the years had predominantly been on the sports outcomes aspect of National Curriculum physical education; that of acquiring and developing skill. There were only two school clubs offered to pupils, both of them for Year 6: netball for girls and football for boys. There was a lack of coherence between curriculum and out-of-hours learning, as there was no opportunity to pursue activities such as gymnastics and dance. The coherence was lacking even in the area of games in Year 6 because of the offer, which was restricted to invasion games only.

The strategy

Through targeted focus-group discussions, pupils were given a voice. Pupil representatives from all year groups were invited to a healthy buffet lunch to talk about school sport–club links and the physical education curriculum in general. Children did not know about the four aspects of National Curriculum physical education, which had formed the National Curriculum process model of education for primary schools since 2000[13]. In developing a strategic awareness, the PLT wanted the children to be aware of these four aspects and for them to permeate all of the learning in the selected areas of activity. The teacher shared the importance of the PLT's role in developing these process skills with learners, especially with regards to evaluating and improving performance. This approach helped the teachers promote continuity and coherence, and, therefore, greater relevance in the programme. Instead of units of work such as games and gymnastics being perceived as separate entities, pupils were encouraged to see progression as opportunity to develop the four aspects further in a contrasting activity. Coordination, control and fluency, for example, were improved in a games context following a unit on gymnastics. Decisions about movement in space in relation to others continued from compositional ideas in gymnastics to tactics in netball. Teachers and learners found the two aspects related to fitness and health, and evaluating and improving, were the most straightforward to connect.

The PLT and other teachers also worked closely with the school sport coordinator (SSCo). School sport was better coordinated and links were developed with local clubs and the sports development unit. This resulted in various opportunities being offered on a rotational basis for different year groups. Coaches worked with pupils who were also invited to join local clubs in the vicinity. The PLT and SSCo provided professional development for the coaches so they knew and were able to refer to the four aspects. The teachers, pupils and coaches produced a poster to show the coherence of the physical education and school sport curriculum offer and how this also linked with local clubs in the area.

Strategic Awareness, Changing and Learning, and Creativity

The challenge

A teacher starting a new job at a primary school found that Year 2 learners were unaware of what the letters 'PE' stood for, they didn't know how they were assessed in physical education and they were lacking in ideas. From the discussion it became apparent that assessment was something the teacher did and pupils equated being 'good at physical education' as being 'good at sport' even though they were unable to articulate what being 'good at sport' looked like beyond 'scoring lots of goals, baskets, points or runs'.

The strategy

The teacher wanted to integrate Assessment for Learning (AfL) principles into her physical education programme and engage learners in peer- and self-assessment as part of the evaluating and improving aspect. In each of the subsequent dance lessons she taught, the outcomes were displayed in the hall to make pupils aware of the aspects of learning they related to. She ensured the tasks she set were plainly linked to eliciting the learning she wanted to

see and clearly shared criteria with learners through her own demonstrations, video or feedback. She drew most of her ideas from the Qualification Curriculum and Development Agency (QCDA) core task pack. She worked with the groups to discuss the tasks and further explored quality and what a successful performance would look like, posing probing rather than prompting questions. Pupils were asked to target such things as how long they would take to learn certain movement phrases, to talk about their feelings during the learning episode and to develop their own ideas. Pupils were regularly asked to monitor whether they were still on track. They were asked to consider the things that helped their learning and things that inhibited progress.

In English lessons, children were asked to keep a learning diary of their feelings throughout the unit and the teachers' lessons were observed by the PLT. Feedback provided included reference to the high quality teaching and learning, taking into account learners needs; the positive engagement of boys in the dance unit; the progress made, which was beyond expectations for a Year 2 class; the quality of dialogue between learners in improving each other's performance; and learner imagination in creating and composing phrases of movement as part of their dance performance.

Changing and Learning, and Resilience

The challenge

Staff at a small primary school were concerned they had insufficient evidence of progress against the 10 outcomes of high quality physical education. It was reasoned that this was because they had not effectively communicated the outcomes. Staff decided they also wanted pupils to have a better understanding of the five outcomes linked to progress and achievement, and to connect these more directly to the five outcomes linked to personal development. For example, they wanted learners to make connections between their desire to improve and their skills, or make connections between their commitment and their fitness and health. They wanted their learners to use these connections to change their approach to learning in physical education, not to give up on certain tasks and stick at learning when it became difficult.

The strategy

The afPE high quality physical education poster[14] delineating five high quality physical education outcomes relating to learners' personal qualities/personal development and five high quality physical education outcomes relating to learners' achievement, focused staff discussion and helped to promote their strategic awareness because of its links to Ofsted criteria and the Every Child Matters (ECM) outcomes. The 10 high-quality physical education posters[15] were displayed in the main hall; the school also printed additional copies to put on view in corridors and classrooms and reference was made to them each lesson. Discussion often centred on what children were doing to achieve higher quality in their performances and teachers reported better engagement from the pupils who felt they could grow and learn better. This belief not only fostered an increased commitment to learning in physical education, but a capacity to stick at learning when it got difficult. In reviewing progress, staff felt this approach helped develop the focus for their questioning and feedback, which was far more pupil-centred and this also helped learners build capacity for a positive approach to learning.

Changing and Learning

The challenge

A primary school wanted to use the seven dimensions as the basis for raising learner awareness, promoting confidence, advancing engagement with the subject matter content and achieving deep learning. The teachers wanted the learning ethos of the school to be developed so that everybody saw themselves as learners, that it was okay to fail and learn from failure, and that effective processes of learning should have a more in-depth focus and were more important than a focus on the product. They wanted pupils to be able to communicate more effectively in the language of learning, to use metaphors, understand the terminology and be able to reflect on the process they were going through. In terms of the seven dimensions, the

school wanted learners to know their strengths and be able to identify the areas that would benefit from further focus. Above all, they wanted parents to be involved in their children's learning to a greater extent.

The strategy

The school labelled its approach **learn to talk**. It started with children in Reception, Year 1 and Year 6. The early years were chosen because they felt it would have the most impact and they also selected Year 6 because the local secondary school was implementing a Learning to Learn approach starting with its Year 7 intake. Teachers decided to ensure their talk focused on learning and, to help this, substituted the word 'learning', where applicable, in any relevant phrase. They rewrote units of learning, classrooms were called learning areas and Year 6 had a **home learning programme**. Home learning involved discussions with parents, projects, watching TV programmes with parents, and literacy and numeracy tasks all made relevant by links to everyday life events. The school reward system was adapted to link to the seven learning dimensions. Pupils received stickers for demonstrating effective learning behaviours as opposed to doing as they were told first time, for sitting up straight ready for circle time or for their efforts in physical education. They would receive stickers for being creative, resourceful and resilient in their learning, even though they may not have fully completed a task. Class totals were monitored to inform the even-handed recognition of, and the even-handed opportunity provided across, the seven dimensions. This was undertaken in all subject areas and physical education offered significant opportunity to contribute to this work.

The same school also awarded badges that read: 'Ask me what I did to get this badge', replacing previous 'well done', 'tick' or 'thumbs up' stickers. The idea was to **promote discussion** about learning.

Parents, in particular, saw value in this approach and engaged far more in their children's learning, enthusing about it at parent's evenings. Performance data following the first year of implementation indicated that the biggest

---

[14] See Further Reading for details of how to download this poster.

[15] See Further Reading for details of how to download these posters.

benefactors were children who had not made as much progress prior to the pilot. Boys' writing had improved significantly and literacy progress was beyond expectations.

Strategic Awareness and Creativity

The challenge

A Year 5 teacher was concerned that, when discussing work with pupils in gymnastic activity lessons, they appeared uneasy with the task, were unable to explain the stage of learning they were operating at and, of most concern to her, were lacking in confidence and unwilling to share what they were feeling when going through the process. She wanted them to be able to talk more readily about the process they were going through, particularly when they were being introduced to new areas of work and involved in composing sequences.

The strategy

The teacher used a 'thinking thermometer' and a 'feeling thermometer', fixing them on the wall when participating in gymnastic activity. Pupils used the thinking thermometer to indicate the 'level' of thinking challenge with regard to the composition task for their sequences; and the feeling thermometer to indicate how they felt about performing certain aspects of the sequence. Each pupil had designed and drawn a character with their name on it in their art lessons and attached them to the chart. At certain points, learners were requested to reposition their character if appropriate. The teacher used this information to ask further enquiring questions and introduce relevant vocabulary. She also used art lessons for pupils to compose sequences of movement. Learners were asked to stick three digital camera images of balances taken during physical education lessons onto poster paper. They then stuck artwork images they had created of two travelling movements that would link the balances. This work was informed by gymnastic pictures sourced from books or the Internet. In physical education lessons, learners attempted their sequences and changed the order by rearranging the sequence or swapping elements with another group to improve compositional fluency.

Signs of success included the quality of engagement with the compositional selection of skills and ideas during the art lesson. The teacher felt this approach helped the insecure performers feel more involved and more self-assured when performing the planned sequence. She also felt children's creative ideas were enriched because they had more time to think about the sequence and progress ideas.

Meaning Making and Learning Relationships

The challenge

A primary school was concerned that children did not associate traditional curriculum time or timetabled lessons with learning taking place off site or outside of the classroom. The school particularly wanted pupils to make meaning of out of hours learning, external activity and school trips.

The strategy

In athletic activities a Year 6 class engaged in a series of timetabled athletic challenges in the autumn term. They were offered coaching activities after school in the spring term and this progressed to inter- and intra-school competition/festival opportunities in the summer term. The activities formed part of the now obsolete TOP Link programme and were supported by young leaders from the nearby secondary school. This provision was shared with pupils in September so that they could see what the year had in store for them. Not only did teachers observe an increase in commitment to athletic activity, they also reported an increased awareness of roles and responsibilities transferred to learning in other subjects. Examples included greater acceptance of leading, improved ability to work independently and an obvious enjoyment of the social aspect of learning.

In Year 6, swimming lessons were taught by a local authority swimming teacher. Prior to the lessons held in the summer term, the swimming teacher attended a meeting at the school to plan links between lessons and other subjects. During the swimming lessons, the class teacher video-recorded evaluating and improving discussion between pupil pairs, linked to developing the overall timing of the stroke. In English lessons, recordings were played back to the class and the quality of the discussion and feedback was reviewed. Targets were negotiated and set for the following week. Children were encouraged to talk about how they worked with each other and the value of the activities they were experiencing. Continuity and coherence with other physical education activities were explained in terms of the importance of the evaluating and improving aspect, and the individual role involved in promoting learning and performance.

All dimensions

The challenge

A Year 1 teacher wanted to introduce the seven dimensions to her learners very early in their school careers and felt physical education presented an excellent opportunity in which to do this. Due to the nature of the subject, the pupils were excited and keen to take part in lessons, but were not used to thinking about their own or others' learning. They were used to responding to tasks by copying the teacher or doing as instructed, which usually required them to replicate a variety of individual skills or engage in drill-type activities.

The strategy

The teacher used the seven dimensions to structure conversation and promote independent thought in the class about learning behaviour. Examples included: 'Can you explain to me how your group is enjoying sharing thoughts and ideas with other people (learning relationships)?' or: 'This group is sticking at their learning task of practising their sending and receiving skills. It didn't go well at first, but now they are more successful. Can you explain to the rest of the class what you were thinking or how you were helping each other to keep going (resilience)?'

Practical Examples – Secondary Schools

Learning Relationships

The challenge

A teacher had used group work as a regular part of physical education lessons for several years. He believed in the value of such work and the team working opportunities it afforded. After talking to pupils and engaging in more critical lesson reflection, he became aware that simply allocating pupils a group to work in did not automatically mean effective group work would progress in the way intended. He started to observe the dynamics of the groups: how they interacted, who they listened to and which pupils were often 'off task', and discovered that patterns emerged. Someone would usually dominate proceedings; learners became increasingly reticent to engage in group tasks for fear of ridicule from their peers and, particularly with larger groups, he noticed there were pupils who made little or no contribution.

The strategy

The teacher began to direct learners specifically to what they were learning in physical education: how to outwit an opponent in various contexts **in** handball, and what they were learning **through** physical education: developing transferable skills; decision making and evaluating; and improving performance. He then focused on the effectiveness of small and large group relationships and how these dynamics might improve the learning 'in' and 'through'. He questioned individuals as to how they might make more meaningful contributions and informed groups that one individual from the group would be asked to summarise the progress made and they would all be responsible for discussing, deciding and improving tactics to outwit the opposition. Pupils developed better learning relationships within their teams characterised by: improved listening skills, allowing all learners a voice; a willingness to talk to each other and share views; the ability to better articulate learning, progress and set targets; more empathy for other learners; the ability to work with individuals outside of their normal peer group; and an enthusiasm for the tasks set, responding well to teacher intervention or comment. Overall the teacher reported significantly improved interdependence.

Critical Curiosity and Creativity

The challenge

A secondary school teacher was accustomed to her Year 9 pupils exceeding expectation for National Curriculum attainment in physical education. Baseline measurements indicated that while standards were high, on average, pupils progressed 1½ levels across the key stage. The Year 11 GCSE physical education examination results had reached a plateau in the past three years after an initial steep slope improvement from 43% grade A*–C to nearly 65%. She felt that much of this initial progress was achieved by 'teaching to the test' and the use of her experience of how the examination boards operated. However, she felt learners were coasting and expected more. The advent of the QCDA (2007) secondary curriculum prompted her thinking about the personal learning and thinking skills, and wider reading uncovered the principles of Learning to Learn. She believed that although she did a lot for her pupils, they could do a lot more for themselves. She found details of and enlisted on an afPE National College for Continuing Professional Development Learning to Learn course.

The strategy

The teacher tried out some of her ideas with a Year 9 group who were following a gymnastic activity as part of a 'learning to replicate' unit. She created a 'word wall' in the learning space and pupils were expected to develop this as new terminology was introduced, either in timetabled curriculum or out of hours learning clubs. Pupils were encouraged to discuss and unpack the qualitative meaning of words and use them in their evaluating and improving processes. This type of discussion was also promoted as a changing room lesson starter.

She began using video of high-level performance, not for learners to copy, but to promote discussion about 'How do they…?' and 'Why do they do that…?' These question types were used to explore biomechanical principles of cause and effect in movement, encourage curiosity and creativity and develop the five key processes of the new secondary curriculum for physical education.

In GCSE physical education the Year 11 group were exploring contemporary issues. She wanted pupils to think of themselves as 'learning detectives'. 'Why' became a frequently asked question for the group – of themselves, of others and of the teacher. Learners investigated race and gender issues as an 'agency' and viewpoints were debated to judge whether evidence suggested cases should go to court. In other words, opinion had to be justified. All children were fully engaged, were more confident to participate and exceeded her high expectations in both their progress in learning to replicate and their progress in contemporary issues. Due to the success of these pilots, she shared her findings with the department and, in the following school term, this became an approach that permeated all of her lessons.

Learning Relationships and Meaning Making

The challenge

Year 10 learners in physical education were poor at completing their homework. Pupil's paid scant regard to the brief given at the end of theory lessons; instead, they would pack away their books early and begin to sidle out of the classroom. Discussions with a sample of the worst offending pupils indicated that they saw no relevance in a majority of the briefs set as they were 'finish off' tasks or 'learn this for next week' memorising tasks. The teacher wasn't convinced these were the only reasons for non-completion as pupils found it very difficult to work independently of others or the teacher in lessons, preferring instead to work collaboratively in pairs or small groups.

Learning Relationships and Meaning Making

The strategy

An activity called 'checking time' was introduced allowing pupils to ask questions about the homework brief they had been set and ensure that they had all resources available. When introducing this, a 'plan of action' for the first few homework tasks was introduced. Building in this time to lessons meant that the supplementary work was no longer bolted on and, instead, became an integral extension to work developed.

To develop learning relationships within group situations (eg, in a games-related practice) learners were encouraged to use terms of praise such as 'well done', 'that's good' and try to say 'why'. Pupils were encouraged to share what they did not know and ask for the help of others. Where they knew others needed help they were encouraged to proactively step in and give support. Questions were promoted as standard learning practice and soon became an integral part of the group's learning. It was accepted that everybody needed to ask questions if everyone was to be a good learner. Pupils were encouraged by the mantra 'there is no such thing as a stupid question'. The learning groups remained together for a whole term and were asked to suggest a group name or identity – one group chose 'team talented'. After this time, pupils were given an option to change groups or form new ones. A genuine sense of belonging and a real unity developed over the unit, which the teacher felt cemented the learner's commitment and engagement with the unit content.

Changing and Learning, Learning Relationships, Strategic Awareness and Resilience

The challenge

Pupils appeared to enjoy their physical education lessons at Key Stage 3. They took care of their appearance, always brought their kit and made expected progress against standards. In Key Stage 4 new activities were offered and pupils could elect to follow two activities.

Some learners were in mixed groups for the first time, others were engaging in activities they had never tried and the teaching and learning approach was very laissez-faire. Learner behaviour and attitudes began to deteriorate. These circumstances had become 'normal' and had continued for a number of years. Pupils were not assessed against standards at the end of Key Stage 4, so the department did not have any measure of learner rate of progress, nor the effectiveness of its teaching, compared to Key Stage 3. Following an incident where a non-specialist teacher threatened to refuse to teach 'options' for the physical education department, staff met to review the situation. Pupils were involved in discussion during lesson time and teachers fed back this information as part of the review process. It was decided that the transition from Key Stage 3 to Key Stage 4 was too much of a contrast and transition for pupils. They went from being spoon-fed at Key Stage 3 to open choice and game playing with little focused teaching and learning at Key Stage 4. Some teachers felt that the gender issue could be addressed and many pupils described feelings of engaging in meaningless activity that was leading nowhere. For other pupils, it became apparent that they didn't feel confident making their own decisions, were afraid of ridicule, and were not willing to take any risks.

The strategy

In developing medium- and longer-term strategy, the department staff decided that at Key Stage 3 pupils needed to be provided with more opportunity to make decisions, take responsibility and develop physical and mental capacity. They also decided to make representation to the senior leadership team of the school for an additional specialist to help with high quality teaching and learning at Key Stage 4 and discuss further the possibility of mixed physical education in Key Stage 3. Finally, they identified the Key Stage 3/4 transition as an area to review and plan for more thoroughly to promote a coherent 11–19 curriculum provision. These actions would help changing and learning, learning relationships and strategic awareness. In the short term, teachers worked as a team and with pupils to address the culture of low expectations. They collaboratively set short- and medium-term learning dimension targets and physical education performance targets. Learners were also asked to develop a series of mottos or sayings that represented their views of physical education at Key Stage 4, but also their aspirations. Some of these were produced as posters and these were displayed in the physical education office and learning areas as aides to memory. A selection of these read: 'Progress without direction is boring'; 'We like challenge'; 'With glowing hearts we engage in dull physical education'; 'Bouncebackability isn't just for champions'; 'Don't just do IT, do PE'; 'Can do'; 'Anywhere, anytime, any task – towards excellence'; 'Not for Sir, but for self'; 'Easy targets, boring lesson'.

The department focused on providing challenge and utilised the pupil's obviously determined aspirations in focusing on the resilience dimension.

Changing and Learning, Meaning Making

The challenge

GCSE examination work had become quite mundane for both teachers and pupils. The content was tackled on a week-by-week basis and this isolated, 'teaching to the specification' approach was unhelpful for pupils. Learners found it difficult to make coherent sense of the various syllabus elements and did not appreciate the progress they were making.

The strategy

Teachers reviewed their approach to the content and piloted an athletics project with Year 10 learners, which integrated theory and practical elements. Staff also sought to link the content to learning in core physical education lessons. For Year 11 pupils, teachers revisited their very early work in Year 10. The pupils, were very surprised to notice how at ease they were with this previous learning and how more readily accessible it appeared. They were asked to reflect and talk about how they felt at the start of the course and many shared confused or worried feelings. Pupils were encouraged to think of their brain as a learning

muscle – it can ache in the same way as muscles can ache following exercise. Regular resting or reviewing can help improvement. Pupils were requested to keep a reflective journal of their 'learning feelings' and progress made over the next half-term. This helped learners monitor their changing and learning.

Meaning Making

The challenge

Teachers in a secondary school were concerned that they were not fully engaging learners in the five key processes of the physical education curriculum. They felt that these were not fully appreciated by pupils, due in part to the teachers' over-emphasis on developing skills in their teaching. Pupil-speak around content promoted the language of sport, but not the broader language of physical education. Teachers felt that this resulted in students unable to fully understand what it is to be physically educated.

The strategy

The teachers started to make frequent reference to the National Curriculum physical education process model of learning. They unpacked the five key processes and their inter-relationship over time with pupils. Staff continuously co-explored, through dialogue and practical experiences with learners, what it meant to be physically educated and how the five processes were promoted through a broad and balanced physical education programme. As a result of this approach, learners who previously perceived themselves as 'no good' at certain sports, engaged in activities to a greater extent, and the continuous dialogue with pupils produced feedback and countless suggestions that contributed to the department review and curriculum design and planning.

Learning Relationships

The challenge

Teachers wanted to promote the use of personal learning and thinking skills in their joint working on a Year 7 healthy active lifestyles project. They were very concerned that the content matter and the pedagogy should not replicate 'the same way of working' as previous project coordination, whether across timetabled curriculum subjects, or organised as project days or project weeks. These prior approaches hadn't produced any impact in terms of improved outcomes for children.

The strategy

Frequent opportunities were planned for teacher collaborative learning and this approach to interdependence was paralleled with pupils even in individual activities. Teachers enjoyed discussing opportunities with other teachers and pupils. Feedback was provided to pupils through guided discussion on how well they had worked together in a group, and links were made as to the impact this had on their engagement with the content and the obvious learning gains made. Of particular note was the plethora of examples that were highlighted relating to the three new aims of the curriculum. Teachers also reviewed their collaborative practice and evaluated the impact this had on their outputs – in particular, the increased range of pedagogical practices utilised.

Meaning Making

The challenge

Teachers wanted to take advantage of the opportunities presented by the new secondary curriculum. In particular, they wanted to explore links between subjects in supporting everyday learning. They believed that this type of work would help pupils see greater coherence between lessons.

The strategy

Year 9 pupils in football and netball recorded data about their game play. This included information such as successful pass percentage, assists, shots on/off target and interceptions/tackles made. Cross-subject opportunities were built in for pupils to engage in an extended 'research task'. The data was analysed in mathematics lessons and presented as graphs in ICT lessons. The statistics were

scrutinised in terms of the tactics each team might employ in the following weeks' games. This work was extended for some individuals into writing a game plan in English lessons or as home learning tasks.

Learning Relationships and Resilience

The challenge

A football coach was trying to help players develop an appreciation of each person's role within the team and the associated pressures or challenges presented. The coach realised that the very nature of the sport can often result in players becoming quite egocentric so he wanted to develop a sense of team empathy.

The strategy

Players were asked to discuss their team roles with other team members. Goalkeepers were in groups with attackers and midfielders were with defenders. Further discussion was promoted by asking the question: 'Who has the most important role?' Over a series of training sessions and games, covering a 12-week period, the attitude and behaviour of the team developed considerably. Of key significance was the increased incidence of praise and support between players and the resulting shared determination when play wasn't going in their favour. Pupils reviewed their performances over the season and, apart from the evident improvement in their win/loss record, also discussed their personal development and increased awareness as learners and the potential for this to be applied to learning in a variety of contexts.

Practical Examples – Further Education (FE)

Resilience

The challenge

A sports course leader had, over a period of time, developed a very good working relationship with tutors at the local university. This was largely due to the amount of students who transferred between the two establishments. It was noted that after transferring, many of the good students struggled to successfully complete the first year of their undergraduate programmes.

The strategy

FE and higher education (HE) sports course leaders met together to discuss the issue and realised that the key difficulties were the increase in autonomy and the level of analysis required at undergraduate level. The nature of the topics being studied for the Level 3 qualification often resulted in 'spoon-feeding' students to meet the criteria for their course rather than working through problems and thinking critically and independently. It was agreed that the assessments and activities offered to the students would be more challenging and promote the processes of a successful learner journey rather than simply ticking boxes of competence when achieved. Some of the learning tasks were deliberately set at a difficult level so learners would experience getting stuck. Staff would then work with students so that they didn't perceive this as failure, rather a challenge to address in terms of getting learning started again. The university tutors also visited the college to help with the teaching and learning of students and this also helped the university staff get to know some of the students who would eventually join the undergraduate programme.

Meaning Making

The challenge

A lecturer wanted to introduce the concepts of sports science in a way that helped to identify the importance of areas such as biomechanics, physiology and psychology. Previously they had been introduced as separate entities, related to the units of study from the examination specification.

The strategy

Students were asked to share their experiences in sport and the level at which they had engaged. They were asked to discuss these experiences and feed this back to the group. Students were then grouped in a 'best fit' way

according to the sport they had the most interest in and were required to produce mind maps. This involved selecting a top-level athlete who represented their sporting group and visually displaying the physiological, psychological and biomechanical attributes required to reach this level. Links were then mapped between these and the seven dimensions. Each time a new module or assignment brief was introduced, these mind maps and mind mapping became a way of scoping the bigger picture context. Software was purchased to allow groups to do this electronically. At the start of each brief, in order to ensure that the rationale was contextualised, the session started with 'What matters to me about this is….' This allowed learners to fully explore the reason they were being asked to do the work and the links it had with other areas of study.

Changing and Learning

The challenge

In an FE setting, a team of tutors believed that students were not taking enough responsibility for their learning or developing themselves as learners. Students were not aware of their own strengths and weaknesses as learners and it was considered that they would struggle to take their learning to the next stage, particularly those entering the demands of HE. After some in-depth discussion reflecting on the plateauing of student results and constricted, uninspiring assessment items, it was decided that the competency- driven content and associated assessment items had negatively influenced the team's pedagogical approach.

The strategy

The tutor introduced the students to the seven dimensions of learning power and worked with them to complete an online profile. In order to develop as learners in each of these areas, it was felt that students needed to develop understanding of the dimension in the type of detail that would encourage it to be part of their learning vocabulary. To achieve this, students worked collaboratively to identify high-profile sports stars who possessed each dimension.

They finally agreed on seven sportspeople whose composition best represented the characteristics for each separate dimension. The sports stars' images were each incorporated in a separate poster with their key characteristics highlighted. These were displayed in various seminar rooms.

The tutor input with regards to the seven dimensions and the completion of the online profile were highlighted in a majority of students' evaluations as a key motivating factor for learning. Students, and perhaps just as important, tutors, became aware of the nature of 'learning about learning' and recognised their roles within this paradigm. This led to a belief among learners that they could change and learn better, and although the competences and the assessment items were set in stone in terms of the module, the teaching and learning developed so that competences and assessment weren't solely the learning drivers.

Practical Examples – Higher Education (HE)

Critical Curiosity

The challenge

Sports studies students in a HE institution were learning passively. They arrived at lectures prepared to be presented to and viewed PowerPoint slides, often printing out the handouts from the institution's web platform and making annotations on the notes page. The routine was pretty much the same for all classroom/lecture-based activity. The majority of students attended the institution's minimum attendance requirements and a sampled survey across faculties indicated students would select modules according to the method of assessment – avoiding examinations wherever possible. They were driven by assessment and only interested in ensuring they had enough information to pass the module and get through the course.

The strategy

In addressing student engagement, a group of lecturers shared ideas as to how they might promote learners who were curious to find out things, were more inquisitive and were generally more active in their learning. Students were encouraged to make notes in new and innovative ways. Mind maps, trees with branches, meaningful symbols, sketches and Venn diagrams were promoted. In module guides the learning outcomes were written in such a way that would allow students to respond in non-traditional ways. For example, instead of the standard assignment format, students were permitted to write in a cartoon, story book or news article format. Students were expected to carry out inter-session tasks in preparation for lectures and at the start of lectures, the focus for learning was shared as a question to provide a hook for engagement; for example, 'What are the similarities and differences between teaching and coaching?' as opposed to 'By the end of the lecture you will know similarities and differences between teaching and coaching.' This approach not only focused students on responding to a problem, but also helped staff frame outcome-driven tasks and plan content in a more engaging and memorable way.

Key improvement indicators included: an increase in overall group attendance (although there were still individual variances) and average pass marks; and students asked more questions and began to suggest ideas for further improvement. Learners demonstrated a greater awareness of their personal contribution to learning, and reflection on this aspect was recorded in the students' Personal Development Planning portfolio.

Strategic Awareness

The challenge

A university wanted to ensure that students understood and engaged in the learning process at the very start of their courses. Previous experience indicated that students would arrive expecting considerable direction in their learning, and lacking the skills to become effective learners. They also believed that this contributed to high dropout rates in the first year of the undergraduate sport programme.

The strategy

The university tutors began their induction discussing Kolb's (1984) Learning Cycle and Bloom's Taxonomy in terms of raising students' awareness about engagement in their learning. A pilot group of students was asked to keep a record of the type and nature of learning activities they encountered and rate these on a 1–5 scale in terms of how the tasks promoted 'bigger picture thinking' and how they felt about engaging in the tasks. There was a high correlation between the thinking promoted and how students felt about themselves as learners (there were a lot of higher order questions/tasks engaged with throughout the semester 1 modules).

Changing and Learning, and Creativity

The challenge

Staff at a university realised that, despite valuing a diversity of teaching, learning and assessment approaches (and attending many such courses sharing the rhetoric), their modules had changed very little over the years and looked very similar in nature. There was little in the way of student involvement in the planning process and the lecture/seminar format still dominated most modules, even when students had reported this to be in need of development over successive module evaluations.

The strategy

Staff at the university referenced the module learning outcomes and discussed indicative content with the students who would achieve the intended learning. Students were encouraged to suggest 'routes through' the content and preferred methods of engagement. This was agreed by staff and students, and greater ownership of the module ensued.

Learning Relationships

The challenge

A university tutor of a research methodology module where the pass rate was consistently below 30%, shared this information with his students. He believed that the nature of the work covered would be better served in terms of achievement if students could develop better learning relationships

The strategy

Having agreed to pilot a different approach, the students were placed in groups of four, where the lowest individual mark on the module for that group would be allocated to all four individuals. This condition led to students meeting in their allocated groups outside of lectures and engaging in peer coaching to help members of the group with learning they found difficult, as well as a dramatic improvement in attendance. Regular conversations about the 'way of working' became a feature of the module. Everybody passed!

Reflective Activity

The purpose of this activity is to consider the ways in which you currently develop a learner-centred approach and the types of strategies used.

1   List similar strategies you currently use to promote learning.

2   Carry out a brief mapping exercise – do you utilise all of the seven dimensions?

3   How does your practice reflect learner needs?

4   What are your key actions for communicating – sharing criteria, feedback, questioning, or peer- and self-assessment?

5   How do your current methods promote deep learning? What is your evidence for this?

6   Explain how coherent your approach is. Ask learners if they are aware of the strategies you employ – what do they think?

7   To what extent are your learners involved in their own learning? Describe some of the learning activities they are engaged with as opposed to the learning tasks.

Further Reading

Websites:

afPE High Quality PE poster mapped to Ofsted Criteria and ECM:
www.education.gov.uk/publications/eOrderingDownload/HQ-P.pdf

Bloom's Taxonomy:
www.learningandteaching.info/learning/bloomtax.htm

Definition and Selection of Competencies (DESECO):
www.deseco.admin.ch/

ELLI: www.ellionline.co.uk/

Kolb's Learning Cycle: www.infed.org/biblio/b-explrn.htm

QCDA High Quality Physical Education Posters:
http://webarchive.nationalarchives.gov.uk/20100209091812/qcda.gov.uk/803.aspx

QCDA Personal Learning and Thinking Skills (PLTS):
http://curriculum.qcda.gov.uk/key-stages-3-and-4/skills/plts/index.aspx

© Alan Edwards

The benefits of a school joining are as follows:

- Regular subject-focused updates via afPE's high quality professional journal – *Primary Physical Education Matters* – three copies of each issue

- Health and safety advice and support

- Monthly e-newsletter and regular email updates

- Access to current and developing specialist subject knowledge and expertise

- Access to a dedicated website designed to support specialist subject knowledge and skills

- Access to publications and teaching and learning materials at discounted rates

- High quality continuing professional development, including subject-specific conferences at discount prices

- Curriculum development and subject leadership – afPE engage with government bodies and policymakers, promoting subject-specific support

- Monthly edition of *Future Fitness* – a sport and fitness magazine

- Certificate of membership.

For more information on afPE Primary School membership, please contact the Membership Department on **01905-855 584** or email **membership@afpe.org.uk**

Physical Education – The Heart of School Life

afPE Primary School Membership
Application Form
(Please print clearly)

Name of school:

Lead contact name:

Title: Mr ◯ **Mrs** ◯ **Miss** ◯ **Ms** ◯ **Other** (please specify):

Role/position:

Address:

Postcode:

Telephone no: **Email address:**

Annual Membership Subscription Fees

The annual fee for Primary School membership is £50.00

Payment Methods

Invoice request ◯   Cheque payable to afPE enclosed ◯

Credit card payments can be processed on the afPE website (www.afpe.org.uk) or by calling the Membership Department on **01905-855 584.**

Please send this form back to:
afPE, Room 117, Bredon, University of Worcester, Henwick Grove, Worcester WR2 6AJ
Tel: 01905-855 584 **Fax:** 01905-855 594
Email: membership@afpe.org.uk **Website:** www.afpe.org.uk

In order to preserve the condition of this resource, please consider photocopying this page.

association for **Physical Education**
www.afpe.org.uk

afPE Secondary School
Membership

The benefits of a school joining are as follows:

- Two copies per issue of afPE's journal – *Physical Education Matters*

- Monthly e-newsletter, text messaging service and regular updates/newsflashes keeping members up-to-date on the latest developments within the subject

- Technical advice to support the safe delivery of physical education and school sport

- Access to Members' area of the afPE website including health and safety FAQs and afPE position papers

- Monthly edition of *Future Fitness* magazine

- Access to the relevant Regional/Home Country Network

- Discount for three colleagues to attend one afPE continuing professional development event or conference per year

- Certificate of membership

- Option to buy afPE's peer-reviewed journal – *Physical Education & Sport Pedagogy* – only available to afPE members.

For an additional £50, schools can access:

- full health and safety advice
- advice on safeguarding
- advice and support following incidents
- support regarding employment law issues.

Physical Education – The Heart of School Life

afPE Secondary School Membership

Application Form

(Please print clearly)

Name of school:

Lead contact name:

Title: Mr ◯ Mrs ◯ Miss ◯ Ms ◯ **Other** (please specify):

Role/position:

Address:

Postcode:

Telephone no: **Email address:**

Annual Membership Subscription Fees

Schools with up to 849 pupils = £115.00 ◯

Schools with more than 850 pupils = £145.00 ◯

Additional fee to include advice/support about health and safety, safeguarding, incident support and employment law = £50.00 ◯

Subscription to the quarterly *Physical Education & Sport Pedagogy* journal = £40.00 ◯

Payment Methods

Invoice request ◯

Cheque payable to afPE enclosed ◯

Total submission membership fee: **£**

Credit card payments can be processed on the afPE website (www.afpe.org.uk) or by calling the Membership Department on **01905-855 584**.

Please send this form back to:
afPE, Room 117, Bredon, University of Worcester, Henwick Grove, Worcester WR2 6AJ
Tel: 01905-855 584 **Fax:** 01905-855 594
Email: membership@afpe.org.uk **Website:** www.afpe.org.uk

In order to preserve the condition of this resource, please consider photocopying this page.

Notes

Notes

© Alan Edward